will he
really leave her
for me?

UNDERSTANDING
YOUR SITUATION

MAKING DECISIONS
for your happiness

RONA B. SUBOTNIK, L.M.F.T.,
Bestselling author of *Surviving Infidelity*

Adams Media
Avon, Massachusetts

Published by
Adams Media, a division of F+W Media, Inc.
57 Littlefield Street, Avon, MA 02322. U.S.A.
www.adamsmedia.com

ISBN 10: 1-59337-485-2
ISBN 13: 978-1-59337-485-3

Printed in the United States of America.

J   I   H   G   F   E   D

Library of Congress Cataloging-in-Publication Data
Subotnik, Rona.
Will he really leave her for me? : understanding your situation,
making decisions for your happiness / by Rona B. Subotnik.
        p.   cm.
Includes bibliographical references and index.
ISBN 1-59337-485-2
1. Single women—Psychology. 2. Adultery.
3. Mistresses—Psychology. 4. Marriage. I. Title.
HQ800.2.S83 2005
306.73'6—dc22
2005017399

This publication is designed to provide accurate and authoritative information with
regard to the subject matter covered. It is sold with the understanding that the pub-
lisher is not engaged in rendering legal, accounting, or other professional advice. If
legal advice or other expert assistance is required, the services of a competent professional person should be sought.
        —From a *Declaration of Principles* jointly adopted by a Committee of the
American Bar Association and a Committee of Publishers and Associations

Many of the designations used by manufacturers and sellers to distinguish their prod-
ucts are claimed as trademarks. Where those designations appear in this book and
Adams Media was aware of a trademark claim, the designations have been printed
with initial capital letters.

This book is available at quantity discounts for bulk purchases.
For information, please call 1-800-289-0963.

With love and appreciation
For Norman,
Adrienne, Kenneth, and Debra

Oh dear—from the beginning I believed every word. And so began the seesaw days, up and down, the highs, the lows. The pitter-pat, the weak-in-the-knees, the waiting for the phone to ring.

Gloria Vanderbilt
It Seemed Important at the Time: A Romance Memoir

Contents

Acknowledgments

*I*n writing a book, there are always other people who help bring your "baby" into the world. I appreciate all those who made this book possible. I'd like to thank my agent, Julie Castiglia, for her help and advice, and for her belief that a woman who is involved with a married man needs understanding, and that there are few places she can go to for help.

My appreciation goes also to the many talented people at Adams Media, Inc., for their efforts in publishing *Will He Really Leave Her for Me?* In particular, I'd like to thank my editor, Kate Epstein, who saw the value in helping everyone in the marital triangle, and who saw this book as a way to do so. I also appreciate the excellent editing skills and keen eye of Heather Padgen and Laura Daly. I am grateful to Colleen Cunningham for the handsome design of this book as well to the entire team at Adams Media.

Norman Subotnik, who has been at my side for all of my adult life, has also been there for the writing of this book. He has read and reread every chapter and every change too many times to count. He has given me his opinion and the benefit of his expert advice on writing, with patience and respect. I appreciate his help and support through this endeavor.

I thank my daughter, Debra Tratt, for reading many chapters, and for her valuable insight, and astute suggestions; my son, Dr. Kenneth Subotnik, for reading sections from his point of view as a psychologist and for rescuing me from some frightening computer glitches; and my daughter, Adrienne Sharp for her encouragement when she was busy meeting deadlines for her own book.

I greatly appreciate the suggestions made by my San Diego colleague Sally LeBoy, adjunct faculty member at Alliance International University, whose expertise as a marriage and family therapist I admire. Sally read parts of the manuscript and provided excellent feedback. I appreciate the thoughtful perspective in the area of cognitive psychology of Dr. Gloria Harris, friend, and coauthor of *Surviving Infidelity*.

I am grateful to three friends for reading the book in its entirety and offering the benefit of their views: Betty Lou Poloway (who read it twice), teacher and university consultant; Dolores Okner, whose opinions reflected her excellent professional organizational skills and sense of humor; and Judy Wolfe, an experienced and compassionate social worker who offered valuable, insightful observations.

I also thank Bonnie Kodesch, for sharing her knowledge from her research. I thank as well the many cherished family, friends, and mentors from the past who have been important influences in my life. I remember Dr. John Askin; Dr. Shirley Glass; Evelyn Davis; Sylvia Lavenstein; Shirley Lapides; and with deepest appreciation, my grandmother Rochel Leah Davis.

Introduction

*T*his is a book that tells your story and will take you on a journey, at the end of which you will be able to answer this important question: *Will He Really Leave Her for Me?* Your story is not simple, but complex. I will explain your affair from the viewpoint of everyone involved, answer important questions that concern you, and pose some that you might not have thought of. Your role in your lover's life perplexes you because you are in the shadows, viewing life from a distance, living as a lady-in-waiting, and wondering about your future. Yet, it can bring joy and excitement, and an increase in your self-esteem.

Before you start this journey, a word about the terms I use. *Infidelity* is used to describe relationships of unfaithfulness or betrayal. It covers the situations addressed in this book. For the married man or woman, it is actually an extramarital affair; for the single woman, it may or may not be a love affair. For simplicity, I use *infidelity* and *affair* interchangeably. Affairs can cover all such relationships, including some that are emotional and some that are experienced on the Internet. *Adultery* is known both as a legal and a religious term, and so I have not used it. I have also chosen not to use the term *other woman* except where someone else does. This term is pejorative, and this book is not judgmental.

Your affair will affect all involved and will dramatically change everyone's life. This book will help you cope with these possibilities and teach strategies for the many situations you could face. You will be asked to step back and become an observer of your own life. Such an approach will increase your understanding, help you cope more effectively with your emotions, and promote better decision-making, resulting in an improvement in the quality of your life.

The information you will find in *Will He Really Leave Her for Me?* comes from a number of sources. First and foremost from my observation of the many men and women who have entered my office for the last twenty-three years seeking help about their lives, as well as from the many stories I have heard in the hundreds of groups that I have led over the years. Information also comes from the work of colleagues and the research available on this topic. I use movies, literature, and case histories to illustrate the points I make. In some cases, I have taken the liberty of putting words together from many people and combined them so that even the speakers will not recognize themselves. Information, identities, locations, and facts are disguised so that no one is identified or identifiable. All confidences have been honored.

Will He Really Leave Her for Me? is divided into four parts designed to take you from an understanding of affairs to the possible outcomes and what they could mean to you.

Part I, "Understanding The Affair," begins with four women who are having affairs with married men. At this point, you will begin a process of gathering information, starting with their stories and their expectations. This is followed by an interesting concept of the three components of love, and I will show you how they relate to affairs. Next, you will find out about the four kinds of affairs that people become involved in. Not all affairs are alike, and recognizing the differences is *crucial* for you. The two individuals involved in an affair may not be experiencing the affair the same way. The differences are important to answer your question, *Will He Really Leave Her for Me?*

Additionally, in recent years two nontraditional types of affairs have been recognized. They truly are affairs, but ones without physical touching. Identifying these new types, the emotional affair and the Internet affair, and how they relate to both traditional ones and the concept of love will give you still more information to answer your question.

Part I concludes with the reasons a woman becomes involved with a married man. Knowing what brought you to this romance will help you understand yourself better. Understanding the reasons can be empowering and create more options for your happiness.

Part II, "The Marital Triangle," will present a picture of all three members of this triangle in chapters entitled "About Her," "About Him," and "About You." You will understand the role of the wife in the affair and find the information that will increase your knowledge of her strengths and vulnerabilities. You may find you can assess her independently from what your lover tells you. As you read more about him, you may be able to assess how strong his connection to you really is. You will understand more about his ambivalence, power, control, self-esteem, and how significant they are to your future.

You will learn more about yourself, the nature of the affair, and how it affects you and your perceptions of your partner's behavior. There will be many quizzes that will help you assess important aspects of this relationship, such as whether he is a "poor-risk partner" and if he will cheat on you in the future. You will learn the role that power, self-esteem, sacrifices, and defense mechanisms play in the relationship and, most importantly, how you can tell if his intentions are serious concerning you.

Part III, "The Affair," explains how affairs proceed in predictable stages. You will learn to identify these stages and what they mean to your future. Power and self-esteem change according to the stage of the affair. You will also come to understand the concept of "the Pursuer and the Distancer," its significance, and how you can see it played out in the affair.

Affairs are complex and are not just influenced by the events and lives of those involved in the marital triangle. You may think it is just the two of you in bed, but in reality, the affair involves you, him, his wife, and the generations before each of you. They are all there and they are exerting enormous influence on you. Learning how family emotional life plays out in the relationship will enhance your knowledge of affairs. You will learn the cognitive model for thinking through your reactions, and see how your thinking influences your emotions. It becomes necessary to challenge distorted thinking so that you can improve your mood. You will find two ways to assess the distortions in thinking that can cause many negative emotions. These are tools that you can use to think clearly about the events of your life now and at any time in the future. Everything you learn will be illustrated by many vignettes.

Part III concludes with a means to help you apply what you now know about the marital triangle to your own situation. You will learn how to assess your affair. There will be case studies that illustrate how to do this, and questions and a form to help you individualize this to your particular situation.

Part IV, "Coping with the Decisions," will consider three possible outcomes of the affair, and will help you understand what can be expected from each. The first outcome to be considered is continuing the affair. If this is your decision, you will be presented with situations you will most likely face.

The second outcome is that you marry each other. In the chapter, "You and He Marry," you will be presented with some very serious matters. When an affair changes to a marriage, the relationship changes as well. This book will present new issues that can arise for you and offers you recommendations for getting off to a good start. You must consider both of the families involved and, if there are children, understand their reaction. You will learn the importance of coexisting with his former wife. You will be asked to acknowledge his wife's loss and develop empathy for the enormity of this event in her life. How well you do this will affect your new marriage.

There will be suggestions for safeguards for your future that you can incorporate into your life, now that you are married. One will be a strategy for adjusting to each other as you leave "life in the shadows" and become a couple. Another is how to protect yourself from being the wife whose husband is having an affair.

And, finally, in the last chapter, "If the Affair Ends," we will consider this outcome. If your love affair does end, you will need to heal from the pain. This book will help you to do that. It will also recognize the changes in your life and the impact on your emotions and your dreams when a love affair ends. You will be helped as you cope with your anger and grief. You will be going through a transition with all its ups and downs, and *Will He Really Leave Her for Me?* will guide you and support you as you restructure your life and search for meaning. At the end of this book, you will be able to see a new future for yourself, and you will have acquired the tools to create it.

As you turn the pages, you will experience many emotions. You will feel understood; you will learn new information; you will learn beneficial skills; and you will hear the truth. You will be treated respectfully and helped, whatever the outcome.

As a therapist, I have dedicated my professional life to helping people through their pain to an improvement in their life. I hope when you close this book, I will have done the same for you. I hope you find satisfaction in life, new self-enhancing experiences, and peace.

I will help you through this process.

Rona B. Subotnik
Licensed Marriage and Family Therapist

Part I

Understanding the Affair

Chapter One

Living in the Shadows

Cathy's Story: Watching from the Wings

*B*ob just stepped up to the podium at the company awards ceremony to receive the recognition for the work he has done for the past twenty years. His efforts have culminated in financial awards for top management, employees, and stockholders. He has produced a great product that has won international acclaim. The CEO describes his award-winning work, and Bob accepts the award to cheers and a standing ovation.

Everyone loves Bob, especially Cathy, his administrative assistant, who believes she loves him in a special way, and more so than anyone else at this banquet. Bob is joined at the microphone by his wife, Helen. They hug each other and Bob thanks her for her support. There is more applause as his teenage twin daughters, Lila and Amy, join their parents at the podium. Cathy feels as though she is part of the family. Over the last ten years, she has heard about their life, problems, achievements, and future plans. Bob thanks his staff by name and asks them all to stand for a round of applause. Cathy stands, but with mixed emotion, feeling she should be the one at the podium with Bob.

Cathy wonders if Helen knows that she and Bob have been passionate lovers for eight years. Through those years, she has often spoken to Helen, who is always friendly and courteous to her. Cathy thinks Helen probably does know. But what Helen doesn't know is that Bob has led Cathy to believe that he is going to leave Helen when their twins go to college. Still, it is hard for Cathy to sit there and watch Helen share the spotlight with Bob when Cathy feels she should be at his side. She was the one who comforted him when things went wrong, she knew intimately all the ups and downs of his work, and she believes that she, more than anyone, helped him get where he is now. She thinks of herself as his soul mate in many ways and is well aware of the personal sacrifices she has made to be with Bob, loving him silently, quietly, in secret, and with an aching heart. All the stolen hours after work have made the possibility of marriage, a home, and children (which she is now too old to have) worth the wait for Bob. Yet, she still wonders, "Will he really leave her for me?"

Michele's Story: From the Internet to a Tropical Paradise

At a posh resort in Acapulco, Michele and Skip are having drinks in the garden outside their villa as they sit in the hot tub, smelling the jasmine and anticipating a night of love in their tropical paradise. They have wonderful getaways like this every month. They usually revolve around Skip's business travel. Today there is very little business for Skip to attend to. Their time is spent dancing, dining, and drinking. Skip is married and his wife is at home with their young children.

Michele and Skip have been sharing a secret romance for the past year, but to Michele it seems that they have known each other longer. She thinks it is better than her first marriage, which ended six months ago. She is not sure how deeply Skip cares for her, but if his behavior means anything, she expects Skip will leave his wife and his humdrum world of bottles, diapers, and carpools for the excitement of being with her.

Michele and Skip met in an Internet chat room for married people who were looking for fun. Their relationship developed into something that felt very special. They seemed very close emotionally. They soon agreed to leave the chat room and contact each other through e-mail. Then they went a step closer: in a few months they were in contact by telephone. After telephone sex, it was not long before Skip suggested that they meet at a point midway between their towns.

From that point on, they started having regular romantic getaways. Skip pays for everything. Because they always meet out of town, they feel the chance of discovery is minimal. Like all lovers, Michele believes their love affair is unique and special.

Michele is twenty-eight and knows she is sexy and desirable. She thinks of her life as wonderful. While she loves being the other woman, she also wants to be the special woman on Skip's arm. And she wonders, "Will he really leave her for me?"

Karen's Story: After-School Romance

Miles away, in an elementary schoolyard in Virginia, Ron is about the only father picking up his son when school is dismissed. This has become his responsibility since he works the night shift while his wife, Liddy, works in a doctor's office during the day.

Ron's after-school routine is always the same. Two days a week he picks up his son, Jon, and Jon's school friend, Michael, and takes them home for milk and cookies, and TV. This is their Tuesday and Thursday routine.

But on Monday, Wednesday, and Friday things are different. On those days, Michael's mom, Karen, comes home early from work and they all go to her house for milk and cookies. Instead of watching TV, the boys are outside playing, and inside, Karen and Ron are having sex. It is quick, furtive, and exciting. Karen is a single mom, raising her six-year-old son alone. Ron has become very important to her, so important that she is fantasizing about being married to him, and she wonders, "Will he really leave her for me?"

Joan's Story: Serious Seniors

Meanwhile, in Phoenix, another woman is also fantasizing about being married. Joan is a widow and lives in a planned community for active seniors over fifty-five. She has joined many of the groups offered in her community, thinking it would be a way to fight her loneliness. Her husband of forty-five years passed away after a long and difficult illness. She became friendly with Leonard, whom she got to know in a hiking club and an oil painting class. Leonard was a comfort to her from the start, as they walked together on the hikes and he listened to how stressful the last years had been for her. When the hiking group stopped for breaks, they always sat with each other.

Leonard calls Joan when his wife is not home, and they have long conversations. He understands her because he went through a stressful situation when his first wife died. He, too, was overwhelmed with grief. Because Leonard was a man, he received the attention of the many single, divorced, and widowed women in his community. Joan did not have such support because there were fewer unattached men available.

He married one of these women shortly after his wife's death and soon realized that he was living with a woman he did not love and with whom he had little in common. He was generally unhappy. He sought friends with similar interests just to make it easier to get through each day.

Joan knows that Leonard is from the "old school," as she puts it, and because of religious convictions he does not believe in divorce. She believes he will change his mind because they talk often of life being short. So for now, she enjoys the time they spend together, but wonders, "Will he really leave her for me?"

About Women Having Affairs

The women we have just met want to marry the men they are having affairs with. But the expectations of women having affairs can vary. Some do not want commitment, some do. Some are not sure, and some find that they change their minds after getting to know the man.

The New Other Woman

Sociologist and researcher Laurel Richardson, in her book *The New Other Woman*, describes the single woman having an affair from the in-depth interviews she conducted from 1977 to 1984 with fifty-five women ranging from twenty-four to sixty-five years of age. Richardson outlines the influences that led these women to have affairs, and cites both the sexual revolution and the women's revolution as two factors. Previous generations were financially dependent upon husbands, but the new woman could earn her way and prepare herself for retirement on her own. By the time she became established in her career and was ready for marriage, she was past the age when women married in previous generations. The chance of meeting a husband diminishes as a woman ages, so rather than wait, these women accepted relationships with married men.

Richardson explains that these women often decided to have affairs because there were simply not enough available single men. Furthermore, there were more women than men, so there were fewer available men. Richardson writes, "Women are devalued because there is an excess of them."

Richardson's interviews showed many women were unhappy because of the conflicts related to their lover having a family. Many who fell in love with married men later found that these men were not going to leave their wives. A few who did leave married another woman. This was shocking to the new other woman because the men had seemed so enthralled with their relationship.

In *Adultery*, British sociologist Annette Lawson reported that 10 percent of those having affairs left their marriages for their lover. Jan Halper, psychologist and managerial consultant, bases her conclusions in *Quiet Desperation: The Truth about Successful Men* on interviews of 4,126 business executives age twenty-seven to seventy-eight. Her findings from the in-depth study of forty-three top-level executives reveal that "less than 3 percent have left their wives for their lover." In their book *This Affair Is Over!!* Nanette Miner and Sandi Terri write that less than 1 percent of the men actually left their wives for their lovers. These are the statistics facing the woman who is having an affair and wants to marry her lover.

No Commitment, Please

There are women and men having affairs with the clear understanding that there will be no expectations by either that they will marry. Neither wants an affair with worries, guilt, or demands. Some of them enter into this kind of arrangement because they are satisfied or happy with many aspects of their own marriage and don't want to give that up. They just like the intoxication and excitement of an affair. In *The Erotic Silence of the American Wife,* Dalma Heyn writes about women who believe their affairs improve their marriage and make their life more complete. There are also single women who are having an affair with married men that they do not consider "marriage material," but they have fun and good sex with them.

Other married couples have an agreement to look the other way if one or the other has an affair, in essence giving permission with an understanding that it is not to affect their marriage. This was the case in the movie *Being Julia,* when Julia (Annette Bening), speaking to Charles, with whom she is flirting, says, "Michael [her husband] and I live separate lives. That is why we are so happy."

Commitment, Please

The women we met in the beginning of this chapter want a commitment from the married man with whom each is having an affair. This they have in common, but there are many differences between them. They vary in age, education, background, marital status, in finances, in how they met, and in their personalities. Some women find an affair with a married man solves one problem only to lead to another.

I remember one woman, Mimi, who told me that she decided on an affair with a married man after going to a singles event and seeing her unmarried daughter there.

> "I was mortified. I left quickly before she saw me. Then I began to wonder if I would be with some man who had dated my daughter. It felt too bizarre. So I went back to an old friend who was married and I started seeing him exclusively. I know he is not happy in his marriage, so I don't think I am hurting their marriage. It's already in trouble. Life is hard. It doesn't always turn out the way you want. I've gotten to care about him and I find myself wanting him to leave her and marry me."

Yes, it is true. Life doesn't always turn out the way you want. Mimi was married at a young age and as she put it, "I thought it was forever."

Her husband, she discovered, was heavily into drugs and she left him at the age of nineteen to raise her two-year-old daughter alone. It was a struggle for Mimi. She went to college in the evenings, and at the age of thirty-five felt free to date and to pursue her career more seriously. Mothers and fathers in our modern time can, to their dismay, find themselves in the same social world as their children.

Many of the women in this group are single women who, unlike the women Laurel Richardson interviewed, did not consciously decide to become involved with a married man. They feel that it just happened as a result of their spending time together and finding themselves attracted to each other. There are also married women having affairs with married men who want to marry their lover, but many are afraid to leave their husband. In this situation the woman's biggest fear is that her lover may not divorce his wife and marry her, even after she has left her husband. The single mom who is in love with a married man has the most difficulty maintaining a romance along with the overwhelming responsibilities of raising children, working, and household responsibilities.

Most of the women who want to marry their lover believe they are truly in love with him. Some of these women are not even aware that he is married when the relationship begins; others know from the start but continue, with the goal of taking the husband from his wife. There are, however, some women who deliberately make the decision to have an affair, mainly due to their own emotional needs. For example, some married women have affairs in retaliation for the husband's affair.

There are also women who are involved with a married man and want him to leave his wife, but they are not actually lovers. Joan, the older woman we met in the beginning of this chapter, is not involved sexually, but as a friend. But she wants more than friendship and companionship. She wants to be married to him. She is torn because she is not comfortable with what is happening, and she wants him to be free to marry her. Recently, this is being recognized as an emotional affair, and will be explored more thoroughly in this chapter.

What each woman has in common, besides wanting her lover to leave his wife and marry her, is a life led in secret, in the shadows, "watching from the wings." Some of these women have a sense of shame, mindful of the hated label, *the Other Woman*. There are many questions that trouble them.

- What if others whom I didn't want to know found out?
- What would happen at work if anyone knew we were involved?
- What would my mother think?
- How will this end?

When they think of their lover's children, some feel a sense of guilt, and when they know the wife and she is friendly and kind, they often feel a sense of remorse. If, on the other hand, the wife knows or suspects and confronts her with accusations and anger, in her mind it validates her lover's complaints about his wife. The woman involved with a married man often feels misunderstood, underappreciated, and deprived of much in life. But when she is with him, she feels special, valued, treasured, and sexually desired. When she is not with him, she can feel anger over the situation—abandoned, unappreciated, and forgotten. The most difficult times are holidays, especially Valentine's Day, Christmas, and Thanksgiving. Other situations that are particularly difficult are when he is celebrating with his family—such as his wife's birthday, their wedding anniversary, and family vacations, or events pertaining to his children's birthdays and graduations. If you are this woman, you know that it is hard to balance the ups and downs of life in the shadows. You spend considerable time wondering where he is, if he is thinking of you, and wishing you were with him. You wonder where you fit in. Will he really leave her for you?

Traditional Affairs

A woman who is having an affair with a married man needs information about the type of affair, the reasons for the affair, and answers to questions she must ask herself.

Such an approach is one in which you think rationally in spite of the anxiety you may be feeling about the course of the affair. Most likely, you have very strong emotions and feelings about this important issue in your life, but your best plan is to separate your thinking from your anxiety over your future and to try to understand this situation. You start by knowing that all affairs are not the same and that the differences can be crucial. In *Surviving Infidelity*, affairs were placed on a continuum according to the degree of emotional connection or investment of the husband for the lover. Now we will use this model to understand what this affair means to both of you. This will tell you something about yourself and your lover. You need to know if you and he are experiencing the affair in the same way or differently

The Serial Affair

The first affair on the continuum is the serial affair, which is a series of casual involvements with no emotional attachment to any of the lovers. A man who is a serial lover has many one-night stands or a series of many short affairs. Visiting prostitutes can also be part of the behavior. His affairs occur on a regular basis because he does not have the ability to sustain an emotionally intimate relationship, with his wife or with his lover. Having both keeps him from getting close to either of the women. His affair is another way to distance himself from his wife and, thereby avoid intimacy. Consciously or unconsciously he does not want commitment or intimacy, but he does want the excitement of the moment.

Individuals who fall into this category are poor-risk partners for a variety of reasons. Some may have personality traits manifested in early childhood and continuing throughout life. Such an individual is usually narcissistic and self-centered. He is not concerned with how his behavior affects you. In other words, he has no empathy, most likely because he did not receive any, or perhaps too much, as he was growing up. Some poor-risk lovers can be very charming and easily fool you with what appears to be their enjoyment of life. We've come to think of them as playboys. After the glow of his charm wears off, the women feel disappointment and some experience heartbreak because he gives so little of himself. He gives so little because his energy is used to cope with his anxiety. Those that continue in a relationship with this type of individual need to ask themselves why they put up with such inconsiderate behavior.

Other poor-risk partners may behave in an erratic manner. You can never be sure if he is going to be sweet and loving or angry and mean. This behavior is often the result of his inability to cope with anxiety arising from his own emotional problems. He usually has a history of difficulty in relationships, frequent arguments with friends, and problems on the job. You may feel that you are walking on eggs in your relationship with him, never knowing what to expect next.

The sexually compulsive individual is also one who might be found in this category. From the work and publications of psychologist Patrick Carnes and others who have contributed to our understanding of sexual addiction, we now know that this individual is in pain and feels shame about his behavior. Dr. Carnes describes the behavior as cyclic, beginning with preoccupation with sexual thoughts, increasing anxiety, then sexual relief in some manner, followed by self-recrimination, guilt, and shame—until the cycle once again builds. Some individuals who fall into this category may have been sexually abused as children.

Individuals with such emotional problems need attention, as they are suffering because of them. If, however, you are involved with one, the likelihood of a satisfying relationship is not good.

In the film *Ray,* about the life of Ray Charles, the blind jazz musician, we see a serial lover in the process of selecting a woman for sex. We see him touching the hand of his prospective partner and then running his hand over her wrist and arm to judge her attractiveness. This is shown repeatedly because Ray had many sexual partners. Even though Ray is blind, his primary criterion for selecting a lover is appearance. He has no emotional involvement with the many women he considers and rejects or accepts, and a slender wrist is an indication of her slender body.

The Fling

Further along the continuum is the *fling,* which is characterized by little or no emotional connection. This affair can be a one-night stand or last longer, or a few such involvements over the years. In this arrangement, one person may consider this to be a fling, but his partner might easily misinterpret the affair and feel there is much more of a connection than there really is. One reason for this is that the passion the affair creates is exciting, intoxicating, and raises the self-esteem of each individual. They are creating a world for themselves devoid of the everyday problems of life. He doesn't fall asleep on the sofa after dinner and she doesn't have to cope with an overflowing toilet while one child has a fever, the other two are crying, and all the while she is worried about her presentation at work the next day. The affair becomes an oasis to escape from the mundane into the adoring arms of an exciting new lover.

It is possible that what starts out as a fling changes in character and moves up the continuum to become the next type of affair, which is *the romantic love affair.*

The Romantic Love Affair

There is a great deal of intensity involved in this affair because the lovers have fallen in love and are concerned with how this affair is to be integrated into their lives. Will they marry? Will there be a divorce? Questions concerning family, children, and even finances become paramount to the decision process.

Do you and your lover both see the affair the same way? Or is it a *fling* for one of you and a *romantic love affair* for the other. There are a number of combinations, and understanding them is vital to answering the question, "Will he really leave her for me?" If you are having a romantic love affair and he is having a fling, you are "out of sync" with each other. There is the possibility that his fling will develop into a romantic love affair, but from my observations, that chance is small because for him there is no or very little emotional connection. This may seem perplexing to you because you are aware of his passion, his delight in seeing you, and you carry his words of endearment in your mind when you are not with him. If he is a serial lover and you see this as a romantic love affair, the chance of him leaving his wife is small, because his worst nightmare is commitment. If you are both having a romantic love affair, the chances improve because the emotional connection is strong. That being the case, his connections to his family may also be strong, and many variables will impact his decision. Many are so conflicted by their love for each other, they feel they must make a decision to stay in their marriage or to leave and marry their lover. Others cannot make such a decision, yet still cannot end their love affair for any number of reasons. In such a case, their relationship can go on to become a *long-term affair.*

The Long-Term Affair

In the film *The Pilot's Wife,* written by Anita Shreve, the wife slowly puts together one clue after another, after her husband's death in a plane crash, until it becomes apparent that he was having an affair with a woman in Ireland. The wife flies to Ireland and knocks on the woman's door, and she is greeted by a woman years younger than she. When she enters the house, she sees a little girl, a baby, and a picture of a wedding in a church in Ireland. To her dismay, the pilot's wife realizes that her husband had been living a parallel life, with his young Irish "wife" and their children. Perhaps one of the most stunning blows comes when she learns that his second wife knew all about her and her daughter, and that her husband shared information with his Irish wife that he had not shared with her. It comes as a surprise to learn from the young wife in Ireland that her husband's mother was still alive and living in a convalescent home. It seemed that he had shared more with his lover than with his wife.

In Search of True Love

So, did the pilot love both his wives? There are many concepts about what love really is; each in its own way is helpful and gives us an understanding of what poets, philosophers, and artists have been trying to depict for centuries. The approach that I believe is most helpful in applying to affairs is the triangular concept by Dr. Robert J. Sternberg, in which he identifies three components of love: passion, intimacy, and commitment. Each forms a side of that triangle, and he considers all three necessary for true love.

Passion

The first component of this concept is passion. It is that intoxicating feeling that peaks early and is very intense in the beginning of a relationship. It is usually the first component to drop off, but it can maintain high levels in a successful relationship. Affairs are high in passion, with an intense longing to see one's lover. This is the point at which the lover is idealized. Dr. Sternberg believes passion is like an addiction and, thus, is the motivational component of his triangle. People addicted to alcohol or drugs are obsessed by them. I remember one woman telling me, "I think and think about the drink, I have the drink, I recover from the drink, and then I start again to think about the drink." This is what many women involved with a married man think. He is very much on her mind and she spends much of her time thinking of him, wanting to see him, and then reminiscing about what they did and what he said. She becomes preoccupied with when they will see each other again.

Intimacy

The second component of Dr. Sternberg's approach is intimacy. He is speaking of emotional intimacy, and I shall take the liberty of using that term so that it is clear that it is not physical intimacy. Women value emotional intimacy and treasure it when they find it in their lover. They were encouraged as little girls to talk about their feelings, while little boys were taught to be more analytical. One aspect of the popular television show *Sex and the City* that appealed to women was the close friendship of the women. They shared everything with one another. Each trusted that she would still be well regarded by the others even when she shared her worries, fears, and self-doubts. There are not many men who do that with each other, but when men and women feel safe enough with each other to open themselves up and still be accepted, they are delighted with their experience of emotional intimacy. Intimacy grows steadily and is the second of the components to peak. Dr. Sternberg feels that this is the emotional aspect of the true-love triangle.

There is often confusion about this second component of true love because it is sometimes associated only with physical intimacy. In the movie *The Aviator,* Katharine Hepburn (Cate Blanchett) has a very intimate conversation with Howard Hughes (Leonardo DiCaprio) in which she warns him that they are different from most people. She shares that she is aware of her own eccentricities and his as well, and this could cause them to become the subject of ridicule in the publicity about them. Hughes is quiet and thoughtful before he responds. He, too, is aware of how different he is. He discloses that sometimes he feels like he is losing his mind. Their openness and sharing do not change their feelings for each other. This is a poignant moment of emotional intimacy between two people. At the end of the exchange, they still love and respect each other and they are closer.

Commitment

The third component of the triangle is commitment. Dr. Sternberg feels this is the cognitive part of his concept. Commitment grows more slowly, but can reach the same heights as the other components. It starts at zero and takes a while to grow. When a bride and groom take their vows at their wedding, they are promising a commitment, but in actuality it takes time for it to develop.

While these three components constitute what Dr. Sternberg calls true love, he identifies combinations of them. When commitment and intimacy are present, it is "companionate love"; when passion and commitment are present, it is "fatuous love"; and when intimacy and passion are present, it is "romantic love."

Regarding the types of affairs, anyone who is having a serial affair is not experiencing true love, but passion. There is only one side of the triangle for the serial lover and that is passion. Because of their emotional problems, for many serial lovers alleviating anxiety supersedes passion. The fling is also characterized by passion. It is in the romantic love affair that the triangle is nearly complete. Passion and intimacy are present, but it is the third component, commitment, that is missing. This, of course, is the key to the question, Will he really leave her for me? In the long-term affair, passion and intimacy are present, but the third component, commitment, is problematic. There may be a spoken or unspoken understanding with the lover that their relationship will continue as is, and so it is, in a sense, a commitment, but it does not include leaving the wife to marry the lover.

In *The Pilot's Wife*, do we see a double commitment? He "married" the Irish woman and continued to live with his American wife and their daughter when he was in the United States. The film showed problems with his life in America, so can we assume that a component of true love was missing in that marriage, or that he was a man who could not achieve intimacy. Living with two families was a way to solve this issue for him. You will find a more in-depth look at this film later in this book.

In the film *Ray*, we see a similar scenario. In addition to being a serial lover, Ray has two families, one known to the world and safely ensconced in Los Angeles—his wife and their children—and another, consisting of a "wife," Margie, with whom he has a child. When Margie tells Ray she is pregnant and asks him to marry her, he refuses and tells her, "You knew the rules." When Ray receives a phone call telling him that Margie has died, his wife asks (surprising Ray and the audience as well), "What about the baby?" Ray's wife, like many women whose husbands are involved in a long-term affair, was aware of his parallel life. Ray was a serial lover who could not be faithful to any of his women.

Affair Confusion

All of the affairs discussed so far are ones that you recognize and are clearly defined, but we now know that there are other extramarital involvements that differ from what we have come to think of as traditional infidelity.

Emotional Affairs

Let's listen in on one such situation.

In a dimly lit, quiet restaurant Jeff speaks intensely to Rose, and she listens, smiles, and concentrates on everything he says.

> *Jeff:* I really look forward to talking with you and getting your ideas on all this stuff.
> *Rose:* Well, how's it going?
> *Jeff:* About the same. We just don't seem to connect or to be on the same wavelength. I've given up.
> *Rose:* What did you decide about the holidays?
> *Jeff:* I'd like to stay here, but Lindy wants to visit her mom and I don't think I can stand that. That's a drag.
> *Rose:* What would you like to do?
> *Jeff:* Get away. I don't know—something different. Have a little fun for a change.
> *Rose:* So how can you do that?
> *Jeff:* Well, I can't do that with Lindy. She has her own ideas and she never thinks about me.

If Jeff and Rose were not in a restaurant, you might guess that Jeff was talking to his therapist. Guess again. Jeff and Rose work for a venture capital firm. They have been deeply engrossed in putting together and financing for a new company. Their work often keeps them in the office after hours. They have had many lunches together and late-night dinners over the past few months, and they now know many intimate details about each other's life.

Jeff knows that Rose is lonely. She is an only child, she has had a few serious relationships, and she cannot have children. This makes her very sad and causes her to throw herself into her work. Rose thinks that Jeff is different from any other man she has known because he talks about his life and not just about the stock market, cars he would like to own, or the latest sporting event. She also knows that he has had many problems in his relationship with Lindy for the last five years since his youngest left for college.

Jeff and Rose are having an emotional affair. Their affair is not sexual, but it has almost all the characteristics of a traditional affair. In her book, *NOT "Just Friends,"* psychologist Shirley Glass identifies emotional intimacy, sexual chemistry, and secrecy as the three components of an emotional affair. There is no component of physical sex, but the chance of it is in the air.

Let's look in on Jeff and Rose again.

> *Jeff:* I guess I would have to go to a little island in paradise with
>   someone really interesting.
> *Rose:* Have anyone in mind? (*laughing*)
> *Jeff:* As a matter of fact, I do. (*smiling and winking*)

Jeff reaches across the table and puts his hand over hers. A shiver goes through Rose, just as it has when he has touched her like that before.

> *Jeff:* I would like that getaway to be with you.

He waits and watches for a response. The response is a smile from Rose that gets bigger as he talks.

> *Jeff:* I know this scene. I've imagined it enough. I can see us lying
>   on the beach together, having a margarita, enjoying the sun, lis-
>   tening to the waves, and not thinking about this damn merger.

Jeff and Rose have not had sex with each other, but, unknown to the other, each obsesses about the other. Their work has drawn them together and they have a comfortable intimacy with each other, one that Jeff no longer has with his wife, Lindy. They know each other's concerns, backgrounds, and dreams. They can each feel the sexual chemistry, but neither acts on it; yet they fantasize about it when they are not with each other, and Jeff thinks of Rose when he and Lindy have sex. Their connection to each other is shrouded in secrecy. They don't believe anyone at work knows, and although Lindy doesn't like the long hours, she doesn't suspect that her husband of twenty-six years would be having a romance with a woman of twenty-six.

Rose believes she is in love with Jeff and that her feelings are returned. She wants so much to tell this to him, but holds back. She does not hold back, however, in her private thoughts. She wants him to leave his wife and marry her. It seems a real possibility to her, from all that she knows about them.

Not having sex has not diminished the feelings. They are at a point where their emotional affair could become sexual and, if that were to happen, it would most likely be a romantic love affair. It seems that this emotional affair is about to become a sexual affair because Jeff has started to discuss the problems he perceives in his marriage and because he touches Rose and she does not discourage it. They are beginning to cross a boundary.

Such a scene has become more common now than twenty-five years ago because there are more women in the workplace today than ever before. Social historian Sheila Tobias writes in her book *Faces of Feminism* that in 1950, 34 percent of women were working, and that it wasn't until 1994 that more than half the women ages sixteen to sixty-eight, or 60 percent, were in the workforce. That percentage has been steadily increasing. We would expect that men and women working together would achieve a certain degree of intimacy and respect that would lead to more workplace affairs, and in fact, there have been increases in affairs in the workplace.

In her clinical study, Dr. Shirley Glass reports that from "1982 to 1990, 38 percent of unfaithful wives had work affairs. By contrast from 1991 to 2000, 50 percent of unfaithful wives had work affairs." She writes that it was the first affair for 55 percent of husbands and 50 percent of wives who had workplace affairs. The workplace is a breeding ground for emotional affairs.

Whether married or not married, the woman having the emotional affair can be just as focused about it as is the woman who is having a traditional affair. She may be even more obsessed if they work together, because her contact with him is often more frequent than that of the woman who is having a sexual affair. The lack of physicality does not keep her from fantasizing or wanting him to leave his wife and marry her.

There are some reality checks that will tell you if you are having an emotional affair:

Emotional Affair Checklist
1. You will not talk too much about him to family or friends.
2. You will not share your feelings about him with family or friends.
3. You save special stories to tell him.
4. You start to share very personal information with him.
5. If others know him, you fear that you will bring up his name too much and give away the special feelings you have for him.
6. You are preoccupied with thoughts of him.
7. You fantasize about a future together.
8. You remember personal details about him.
9. You desire him to touch you, to kiss you, to make love to you.

This is also true for him. He is especially on guard not to speak of you to his wife, and the married woman having the affair is just as cautionary.

While Jeff and Rose sit together in a restaurant in Bethesda, Maryland, looking into one another's eyes and wanting very much to be in each other's arms, across the country in Nevada City, California, Sadie is "virtually" in Gregg's arms, although he is in Manassas, Virginia. Here is another type of affair confusion: the virtual affair, not taking place in a dimly restaurant but in cyberspace on the Internet.

Internet Affairs
Cyberspace has replaced older and more traditional ways for men and women to meet. Some describe it as "an Internet cocktail party."

People can develop a parallel life online, living a fantasy that does not relate to their life in real time. It can become very important to them and can be a way to satisfy some of their needs, but at the expense of everyday living. It can create addictive behavior in a population that would not previously have been thought to be at risk.

Psychologist Alvin Cooper, who has extensively researched and written about this new technology, writes of three properties of the Internet that he identifies as very important in understanding the impact of it on our lives. He calls these properties the Triple A Engine. They are Accessibility, Anonymity, and Affordability.

Accessibility

The first of these properties is *accessibility*. The meeting places of the past, like the town square, the mall, the singles bar, and the bookstore, for many have been replaced by this technological wonder, the Internet. The Net is always open, allowing individuals to log on at any time from any location and find someone to talk to. All one needs is a computer, and there is always someone in cyberspace to connect with.

Affordability

The second property identified is *affordability*. Except for the minimal monthly Internet provider service (IPS) fee, there are few charges. If you want to meet someone and you don't want the hassle of going out alone, just boot up your computer and see who is "out there." If you don't like the person you meet, you can end the evening rather quickly with just a click of the mouse. And if you meet someone interesting, there are no expensive dinners, clothes, theater tickets, or parking fees. And forget about a bad hair day. That doesn't exist in the Land of Oz!

Anonymity

The third component of the Triple A Engine that drives the Internet is *anonymity*. With a screen name of your own creation, you can go anywhere and say anything you desire, and no one will know for sure if you are who you say you are. This can be helpful if you feel you are rejected quickly in the real world on the basis of how you look. Overweight people report this happens to them repeatedly offline, but not online. Shy individuals are more comfortable at their computers than they are standing around in "quiet desperation" at a cocktail party. The negative side of this is that people lie or bend the truth, so you can't be sure of the veracity of what you read on the Net.

Dr. Cooper and his colleagues conducted a large-scale questionnaire in 1998 called the MSNBC Online Sexuality Survey, based on the answers of 9,177 individuals who had at least one online sexual experience. The survey gives us much information about use of the Internet. Some findings were that 5 percent of the respondents said they lied about their gender (known as "gender-bending"), 20 percent said they were *often* untruthful about their age, and 61 percent said they *occasionally* lied about their age.

In the film *Closer,* Dan (played by Jude Law) goes online to lure Larry (Clive Owen) to a meeting place by gender-bending. He pretends to be a blond woman, and on the computer types very explicit sexual text that intrigues Larry. The next day, Larry goes to the designated meeting place to look for the "woman" he believes he met online. When he arrives he meets Anna (Julia Roberts) instead. Larry had set Dan up by pretending to be a woman in order to have him meet Anna. It was so easy to do. Larry and Anna enter into a real-time relationship filled with betrayal, infidelity, and demeaning language and behavior toward women.

Individuals seeking to meet someone online have a choice of going to a dating service or to a chat room. There are many dating services, and some have relationship-support components. There is a feeling of more control because of the questionnaire that many provide, but other sites are more like a listing of personal ads. There are hundreds of chat rooms with "themes," many that you probably could not have thought up if you tried. Some are designed around bringing together people with common interests and attracting individuals with sincere intentions to the site. Others are essentially a place to flirt, using a screen name, and no questionnaire; it is mingling anonymously.

Coast-to-Coast Romance

Sadie's alarm goes off at 4 A.M. in Nevada City, California, three hours earlier than she used to awake during the week. But her routine has changed; now she gets up at that time every Monday, Wednesday, and

Friday so that she can IM (instant message) Gregg, who is in Manassas, Virginia. He logs on at about 7 A.M., when his wife is asleep. Gregg is an engineer, married for seven years, and has two children. Sadie and Gregg met in a chat room, but their attraction was so strong and so immediate that they started chatting privately. After a while, they started communicating directly with each other through e-mail.

Sadie's view:

"I know he is truthful because everything he says makes sense and if he were lying, I am sure he would have tripped himself up. We have been together online for seven months. I want to meet him, but he can't get away because of his wife and kids. He's very honest because he told me right off he was married. He e-mailed me a photo of himself. I know what he looks like and he is great looking. We have lots in common. We both live in small towns and we are really cut off from a lot of the social life others have.

"He is really kind and very romantic. He writes things that make me shiver. We've had cybersex and I think he is wonderful. I never knew that could be so wonderful. He has changed my life. I feel alive. Before I had felt depressed. Now I think of Gregg all the time. I want to meet him face to face. Even though we haven't met, I feel I know him and I want to marry him."

Sadie may be right about his honesty, but it is hard for her to tell. Gregg could have sent a photograph of anyone and Sadie wouldn't know.

It does not appear that Gregg is interested in anything more than a sexual relationship online. He may be a serial lover, but more than likely is having a fling, and the component for him is passion. Sadie, on the other hand, experiences this as a romantic love affair. Sadie feels that they have developed a sense of intimacy because he has been open about his marriage. Gregg feels passion and has shared some details of his life, but Sadie cannot be sure if what he says is true or is designed to prevent them from meeting. There is no sign of a commitment from Gregg.

Internet relationships develop very quickly and individuals find that without the deterrents present in real life, they disclose information they would not when face to face. Couples communicating with each other feel alone and develop a special kind of closeness that they mistake for intimacy. For emotional intimacy to develop couples must interact face-to-face in the real world. For real intimacy to develop, they must be able to see each other under many circumstances, know each other's weaknesses as well as strengths, and feel sufficient safety in the relationship to share their deepest feelings.

Another factor in developing emotional intimacy online has to do with projection. One cyberlover can project his needs and desires onto the other more easily than in real time because the blank computer screen makes it very easy to do just that. In fact, it facilitates it. It allows people to fill in the blanks from their own needs and the lover becomes someone else, someone she wants to re-create from other people in her past or someone she has been searching for and has never found. Communication online is fast, eliminating words, and dashing to the next thought. It is also read quickly and is like fast food, missing in flavor.

So Sadie is in this predicament of having been caught in the mysterious ways of the Internet. She is having a *virtual* love affair, but her feelings are *real*. She thinks she is in love with a man she doesn't really know and who appears not to be interested in meeting her, let alone marrying her. It can happen easily on the Net. People report being surprised about how strong their feelings are and how open they become. It is a combination of the psuedointimacy that one experiences online and projecting one's needs onto the blank screen. Sadie's pain will be great when she realizes that she and Gregg will not marry, just as Gregg's wife will be when she realizes that he is online at seven o'clock in the morning, bringing another woman and himself to orgasm by what they type to each other. It is not the same as pornography because instead of staring at a picture, there is interaction with another human being who is responding to what is written, and who in turn does his or her best to bring the lover to orgasm. But for all we know, "Gregg" could be a teenager whose mother doesn't know what he is doing at seven in the morning. Or he could be another woman, or someone thirty years older than Sadie.

At the end of the first workshop I ever held on *Surviving Infidelity* more than twenty years ago, one woman remained after the others had left. She looked stunned and then spoke to me.

We had the following conversation:

They were talking about me.
About you? I don't understand.
I'm that woman they are talking about.
I see you are having an affair with a married man.
Yes.

I thought of the pain that had been in that room a few minutes earlier, the despair these women had felt. I remember, in particular, the hushed silence as one woman spoke about the painful medical treatment she had to undergo because her husband had passed on to her a sexually transmitted disease.

I don't understand. Why did you come?
I need to survive this infidelity, too. I don't really understand.
    How did I get here?

The next chapter will explore this topic. Although you may think you know, it is vital for your own self-knowledge to understand how you got there. If this affair satisfied an emotional need, you need to understand how you can meet that need in a way that brings you happiness, not pain.

Chapter Two

How Did You Get Here?

*B*eth sits in her New York office studying a spreadsheet on her computer. She is preparing for a presentation of a new line of designer shoes for the upscale chain of boutiques where she has worked for ten years. At age thirty-five, Beth is about to move into a top management position. She feels this is a great time in her life.

Linda, across the river in New Jersey, receives a phone call from a motel in New Hope, Pennsylvania, concerning a problem with reservations for the first weekend in October. She becomes concerned when she realizes that is the weekend she and her daughter, Marcie, will be visiting a college in Maine that Marcie had considered applying to. Frantic hours of checking old phone and credit card bills and computer files leads Linda to suspect the reservations are for her husband, Roger, and someone else. This realization is followed by a tearful and angry phone confrontation with her husband, in which he reluctantly reveals the affair. Linda now knows about Beth. Linda and Roger both hang up angrily from their conversation.

Roger, in his office in Manhattan, picks up his phone and places a call to Beth. She looks up from her computer screen, answers the phone, and hears Roger say, "She knows."

There is silence.

"She's in a rage—very upset. She checked all the phone bills and she knows about New Hope."

"Well, so she knows. It's out in the open. We don't have to hide anymore. Now you can tell her about our plans for our future together. This is a good thing, isn't it?"

More silence.

Beth continues, "Well? I'm sorry, but it was going to come out sooner or later. Now it's done."

More silence.

"What's going on, Roger? We can handle this."

More silence.

"Say something, for Pete's sake."

"I don't know what to say."

Beth sighs. "You don't know what to say. I don't believe this."

"Beth, it's not that easy. Linda's upset. The kids will find out. Maybe this is a mistake."

"I don't believe what I am hearing!"

Roger was the intelligent, handsome guy Beth always wanted to meet and never thought she would. And there didn't seem to be many men to choose from. She had never met anyone like Roger, someone she could share with and just be herself. So even though she knew Roger was married when she met him at a sales meeting, she couldn't stay away from him. They had great sex and wonderful conversations. They had agreed that they both wanted to be together and they would be married as soon as his youngest daughter left home.

Beth is confused, hurt, and angry. She no longer knows what is real about their relationship. She wonders how she got to this point.

We know that Beth's need for intimacy was being met by her affair and that her concentration on her career kept her from dealing with her needs earlier in her life. It is important for you, as well, to understand what brought you to this point. The decisions you make and the way you choose to live will benefit from carefully exploring this topic.

The following stories will show many of the reasons why a woman has an affair with a married man. Such situations can be complicated, and at times there can be more than one reason.

Intimacy

Intimacy needs can be one reason for becoming involved in an affair. This was the case with Julie and her husband, Hank. They made an appointment with me to discuss an affair he had had with Ruth, a reporter for a local magazine. Ruth was someone Hank ran into occasionally at business meetings. Julie was recounting the pain she felt from the affair when Hank interrupted to say, "I notice she doesn't mention her own affair."

After learning their history, a complex picture emerged. Julie and Hank had been married for twenty-five years and both acknowledged that they felt their marriage had been falling apart for some time. Hank felt it was because of his long hours at the office, but Julie said that although she wasn't happy with that, she was tired of his being so controlling about almost everything in their lives. They both went on to describe how the situation had begun to deteriorate and that they had sex infrequently.

Then two years ago Hank had his affair.

"It was nothing—just nothing. Ruth meant nothing to me then and she means nothing to me now. Julie means everything to me. That affair only lasted a few weeks, but Julie and I have been married a quarter of a century. I don't even know why I did it. It should be old news now. It didn't happen yesterday. It was stupid."

"When I found out about it, that was the final straw," Julie added.

She went on to explain that as a result of the problems they were experiencing and Hank's infidelity, she had met with a lawyer about a divorce. She began telling her lawyer, Thomas, many personal concerns—more, she realized, than she really had to.

"Thomas made a difference in how I was feeling. He listened to me, and I finally felt understood. I responded to his caring and compassion. At the second meeting, he held me just before I left and it just went on from there. Thomas and I began to meet first for lunch and then at motels. I had mixed feelings about what I was doing. I reasoned that Hank had done the same thing. But that really wasn't it. I liked Thomas's gentleness and how we could talk. It was hard to stop when I felt so happy. I tried to end it on two occasions, but I started it up again."

"I found out about it and that's why we are here," Hank said.

This was a story with a twist. Julie was both the wife and the lover. When Julie told her lover that Hank knew, Thomas backed off, became cold to her, and said he loved his wife and wouldn't leave his marriage. He referred her legal case to his assistant. "It's not that this hasn't been important to me. It has, but I have professional and family considerations," he told Julie.

"When he said that, I felt used," Julie said. "I wasn't sure what to do. Nothing in my marriage changed. In fact it had gotten worse because Hank found out about Thomas. I began to realize how depressed I was."

Eventually Julie and Hank decided they had a lot invested in each other and needed to work on their marriage. Hank was not like many men who leave when they discover their wife has an affair. This took a great deal of effort, but they did reach a point in which many changes were made that improved their marriage.

The appeal of the affair for Julie, just as it had been for Beth whom we discussed earlier, was that someone was there to listen and understand her. This is the type of situation British sociologist Annette Lawson refers to when reporting that infidelity is a greater threat to the marriage when wives are unfaithful than when husbands are.

If he is uncomfortable with intimacy, the wife's affair may satisfy her needs for intimacy that the marriage does not. Since the need for intimacy is so strong in a woman and her marriage does not provide it, once she finds it in her affair, she may be reluctant to give up the affair.

Loneliness

Lisa sat quietly in my office. We were meeting for the first time and she was having difficulty getting started.

"I don't know where to begin."

She started describing behaviors that were symptoms of depression. She had told me she was relatively new to the city, having accepted a position in a prestigious laboratory as assistant to the director in her narrow field of interest.

"I love the work," she told me. "It was a good choice and I was lucky to have landed this job. On the downside, I only know a few people here and I am not a very outgoing person. My hours are long, so I am not meeting anyone. One of the older scientists has befriended me. One day he asked if he could join me at lunch when he saw me eating alone. Even though he is very outgoing and I am not, we have a lot in common. So we began having lunch together almost every day and sometimes he would stop by for a coffee break. Eventually, he started asking me out for dinner, and I accepted."

When I asked Lisa about her feelings for him, she said, "He's wonderful. He has been a mentor at work. We both love opera, and we helped each other with personal problems."

"And," I repeated, "your feelings about him?"

"We have a lot in common."

"He sounds pretty important to you. Tell me how you feel about him."

"I don't know. Well, he's fifty-five. That's about twenty-three years older than I am. He's a young fifty-five, nice looking, and really a gentleman. He has a wife, three sons, and five grandkids."

"And?"

"About a month ago his wife was diagnosed with a strange virus that will debilitate her for a while. He was very upset and he said that he would not be having lunch with me anymore. He no longer stops by. When I run into him at work, he is very polite, just as he is to everyone."

"How are you with that?"

"I think of him all the time. I guess I feel hurt. Even though his wife is sick, we could still have lunch."

"Have you sent her a card?"

"No. How could I do that?"

"Because?"

"Because he's married? What would she think?"

"So, he seems more than just a friend."

Lisa began to admit to herself that she was involved with a married man—much more than she had allowed herself to believe.

"He was my friend. I didn't see this as a conflict with his marriage. I guess he was becoming more important to me than I realized."

Lisa was depressed because she experienced a loss of someone who had come to be very significant in her life. At the same time, she was a newcomer who had done little to become involved in her community. Because of this, she did not have a support system to help her when she needed one. She felt very much alone.

This "special friendship" was an emotional affair and the loss of his attention and participation in her life was very painful. In actuality they had been sharing their private lives with each other and in so doing developed an intimacy that is similar to that of a committed couple. Lisa no longer felt painfully alone.

Not all single women are lonely, and being married is not a guarantee against loneliness. A popular group I led many times was called Loneliness in Marriage. It feels very isolating to live a life with few social and emotional connections.

Collette, a member of the group, had this to say on that subject:

"I feel very disconnected from the world around me. I live with my husband in a small town in a house I inherited from my parents. I work at home, repairing old dolls, making doll clothes, and on weekends selling them at flea markets and craft fairs. I always felt we should move to a bigger town. I'm forty-five, and even though I'm married, have a home, and do something I really love, I feel life is passing me by.

"There's a man from the flea market I am having an affair with. We made a deal that this would have no effect on our marriages. After all, no one knows about us. We meet out of town. But he's come to mean so much to me that I want us to divorce our spouses and marry. He wants to stick to our deal and says we can be happy with that. It's not enough. Somehow I feel hurt and still believe that life is passing me by."

Obviously, Collette, like Lisa, had been looking to the affair to help her cope with her loneliness. It did that. But now it's brought her another problem: her lover doesn't want to marry her.

The Old Flame

Author Anita Shreve, in her novel *The Last Time They Met*, tells of an affair that develops when two former lovers meet by accident. Their romance had ended after a traumatic car accident they had been in years earlier. Even though they were both happily married to other people at the time they met, they had an affair. In the novel, Linda, the other woman, writes a letter to her lover.

"What shocks me is my love for you. I would like to think that what we have could exist outside of real time, that it could be a thing apart and not invade. Foolish and dangerous thinking. It has already invaded every part of my life."

When former lovers or former spouses meet, the feeling, memories, and experiences they once shared and enjoyed come back to their mind. In fact, seeing an old flame can bring back fond and often sensual memories that may compete unfavorably or more favorably with the reality of today. For example, a class reunion often brings a former couple together with a spark they thought had long been extinguished, which confuses them because they are now happily married to others. They may react to the past by having an affair in the present.

Bev and Tony came into my office with a not-so-unusual situation. Tony, like the lovers in Shreve's novel, met his old flame, Liz, by chance when he was attending meetings in Chicago at his company headquarters. They exchanged phone numbers and he promised to call so that they could have dinner whenever he was in Chicago.

Tony told Bev about the meetings, characterizing them as old friends who just got together for old times' sake. Bev voiced no objections even though she really had many. "I wanted to be cool," she told me. Bev came across e-mails that Tony and Liz had sent to each other. Clearly, they were not e-mails from a friend but from a lover. They had picked up where they had left off. Liz wanted Tony to leave Bev, but that was not what he wanted.

Tony, who had been thinking he could handle both his wife and the old flame, became alarmed at how badly Bev and his marriage were being affected by this. Together, Bev and Tony wrote an e-mail to Liz telling her that the relationship was over. When Liz persisted, they put her on their computer's spam blocker. Together, Bev and Tony began the process of healing.

Old flames can meet by accident, as Tony and Liz did, or maybe they seek out the other using the computer and their investigative skills. In these cases, the mind has already conjured up the memories of the past.

Not all affairs with old flames or former spouses end in this manner. Sometimes it is the marriage that ends—not the love affair.

The Tony Soprano Syndrome

In the award-winning television show *The Sopranos*, mafia leader Tony Soprano is one of the most powerful men in town, and he has a bevy of "goomahs" (Mafia slang for the "other woman" or "mistress") that his wife Carmella knows of. Some "goomahs" know the score—that nothing will come of it, but a few fall for Tony. Fans of the show may remember that Tony did not fall in love with any of these women, except Gloria, a beautiful car saleswoman he met when he was shopping for a Mercedes as a surprise for Carmella. Gloria returned Tony's feelings and became involved with him in an affair. Leaving Carmella was not an option for Tony because under his code of behavior the family is sacred. But Tony represents that powerful man that many women are attracted to.

Former secretary of state Henry Kissinger said, "Power is the great aphrodisiac." Some women are attracted to men in positions of leadership who are usually superachievers, competent, charming, charismatic, and admired by many. He might be the president of the United States, a member of Congress, an opera singer, rock star, clergyman, CEO, athlete, or celebrity, to name just a few. Even though he may be married, many women are attracted to him and easily fall into the role of his lover when their interest in him is recognized and returned. They are flattered by the interest of such an important person and feel they are special because of the returned attention. Some come to believe they will be married.

In the report issued by Special Counsel Kenneth Starr, Monica Lewinsky was quoted as saying she was in love with President Bill Clinton, "that he was sort of my sexual soul mate," and that she felt that sometime in the future they would marry. The affair ended sadly for everyone involved. Unfortunately for her and for the Clinton family as well, Monica Lewinsky was a young woman who made her mistakes publicly. Consequently, she was subjected to ridicule rather than having the privacy to understand why she was in the affair and how to resolve the issues that caused it and were caused by it.

While the odds are poor that the powerful man will leave his wife and marry the lover, it does happen. Former congressman Newt Gingrich left his wife and married his lover. In fact, he did this twice, once to his first wife and then to his second. The powerful man usually has a lot to lose professionally when the affair becomes public, but the woman will also have significant problems from the disclosure.

This was the case with Rachel, who was attracted to her clergyman. She attended services regularly and was a very active member of the congregation. Rachel was not a young intern-type, but a mature woman, the mother of two teenagers.

> "I really thought he was in love with me and I believed that because he loved me with such fervor, he wanted to marry me, just as I wanted to marry him. We were drawn together because we were interested in the same issues. He told me how much he admired my intelligence and devotion to worthy causes. I was very flattered, but then we were discovered and my world crashed around me. It became public knowledge and everyone was embarrassed. My children were teased and mortified. My husband felt he couldn't hold his head up. I think he has stayed in the marriage to be there for the children. Our pastor was required to have therapy, was dismissed from the congregation, and sent to Timbuktu or somewhere. It seems I was not the first for him. And I don't know what is going to happen with our marriage. We are living one day at a time."

In the previous examples, neither the lawyer nor the pastor made promises of marriage, but often women come to believe they will marry their lover, either by assumption, innuendo, or by the actual promise of marriage.

The Promise of Marriage

Many affairs are nurtured by the promise of marriage somewhere down the line. For many men, it is a fling of long duration, but for the woman it is a romantic love affair. She stays in the relationship because she is in love with him. Some believe what their lover says, others have doubts, but they all hope he will keep his word. He might tell her of his unhappy marriage, describe his wife as cold and incompetent, and promise that soon he will be free to marry her.

This was the case with Laura, who told her support group that she had been having an affair with a married man for six years. There was a startled silence, and then someone asked, "Well, where is it going?"

"He's waiting for the last child to go to college."

"When will that be?"

"Another five years."

"And how old will you be?"

Reddening and unsmiling, Laura replied, "I'll be forty-two."

"I guess you don't want kids."

"Sure I do!"

One woman ventured to say what everyone else was thinking.

"Laura, maybe he won't marry you. It doesn't sound like he wants to leave his family. What will you do if the last child goes to college, and he won't marry you? You will have given up eleven years of your life, and probably your chance to have children."

Laura was one of the women who enter into an affair because of a strong attraction to her lover, belief in his story of his unhappy marriage, and the promise of a wedding for the two of them in the future.

Some women begin an affair with a man, not knowing he is married. When that knowledge surfaces, so do the promises like his divorcing his wife and marrying her. The right time, he tells her, is in the future, and usually involves an event like a daughter's wedding or receiving a long-awaited promotion. Usually the marriage continues even when that date arrives or the event occurs that was supposed to allow him to be free to marry her. Then he offers another date or reason, and another waiting period.

His marriage continues even though the child graduates, the daughter marries, the mortgage is paid off, or whatever the designated end-point was. In many scenarios, he and his wife have meanwhile made their plans for the next period in their lives. Instead of leaving his marriage, the man takes his wife on a trip to Europe, they buy a second home, or somehow he indicates the marriage is not ending.

For a very few women, there is a divorce, the promise of marriage is kept, and they make a life together. For most women, however, it is an empty promise. Others, sadly, may find that he leaves both the marriage and the affair for yet another woman. When such an ending occurs, the lover feels some of the same emotions the wife feels, such as abandonment, betrayal, and rage.

"How could you do this to me?" she asks. She has invested many important years in this affair and has sacrificed so much for it that she becomes depressed, angry, and bewildered. She has been betrayed. But as the other woman, she gets little sympathy or support. And there are few, if any, people in whom she can confide and share her feelings. She feels very much alone as she tries to cope with his betrayal.

Self-Esteem

In her townhouse in Washington, D.C., Lois sat looking at the numbers in the phone book under Howard's name. Even though their relationship was very new, she missed him and wanted to speak with him. This week he was traveling to nearby Virginia for the opening of his company's newest store. His cell phone was not receiving calls, and that was the only phone he had told her he owned. She was sure he had said he took all calls from his cell phone. On a whim, Lois looked in the phone book and saw his home number. She was surprised to see where he lived. It was an area for young families. He had told her he had a condo in southwest Washington, D.C. She looked again. Maybe it wasn't Howard. It was only a number next to his very unusual last name. She dialed and a woman answered the phone. Lois thought it was a wrong number.

"Is Howard there?" she asked.

"No."

"Oh. Is he at the new store?"

"Yes. Can I give him a message?"

Lois hung up the phone. She was stunned by these events. She wondered who the woman was. Then her phone rang.

The woman at the other end had dialed "*69." When Lois picked up the receiver, she heard the woman saying, "This is Howard's wife. Maybe we should talk."

Lois was too shocked to reply, but too curious to hang up.

"He won't marry you. He doesn't marry any of you."

Lois was devastated by what she heard. Even though she had known Howard only a short while, he had made her feel good about herself, and happier than she had been in years. His attention to her was passionate. He pursued her, and she loved it. No one had ever done that. They had been lovers almost from their first meeting, and her attitude about herself had taken an upward swing in this short time. Only, she didn't know he was married. Even after learning this, she wasn't sure she would stop seeing him. In her heart, she believed they were heading for marriage.

One of the reasons women enter into affairs is that the attention and excitement of the affair make them feel better about themselves. Lois came to a support group to talk about her feelings. It took a number of sessions to speak about her despair at finding out that Howard was married.

"I met him at a bookstore. We had coffee and he took my number. We clicked right away. I thought he cared for me."

But one group member put it well. Diana said, "Honey, you're lookin' for love in all the wrong places. Look inside yourself, doll. You gotta love yourself."

Lois was at that decision point women face when they find out their lover is married and must decide whether or not to continue the relationship. With Howard's history, it didn't look promising. If she had continued, she might have found herself in an affair with the promise of a marriage that was not likely to take place.

Is It Chemistry or Something Else?

When clients start referring to last night's episode of *Sex and the City* in their counseling sessions, it is an indication of how a new generation has grown up with a different attitude toward sex than previous generations. A television program that depicts the life of women in the big city, wearing glamorous clothes, walking about in designer shoes, and having an active sex life is fun to watch. But it doesn't often have much to do with the reality viewers are living.

I find that in groups and individual sessions for premarital counseling, it is rare that a couple is not already living together. This change of attitude toward sex has opened the door for some women to consider an affair. His wedding band may not be a deterrent to an affair without guilt, but his view about marrying his lover may be, if she ends up falling in love with him.

Always On

Gina was vivacious and always laughing. In fact, flirting was almost a way of life with her. She was a woman who was looking for love regardless of whether the guy was married or single.

Gina told her group, "It's just a lark. I like to have fun. I like to feel the energy in a room."

It was this "energy" that Gina needed to keep her going. Inside, she felt empty, lonely, and sad, but these feelings seemed to disappear when she got feedback from a man that she was desirable. He was like a mirror she could look into and see that she was okay. She didn't understand that her behavior was driven by her low self-esteem and reinforced by the response she received from the men she became involved with. She didn't feel guilt or remorse because of the affair because she had no experience with being compassionate or having the ability to see something from another person's point of view. In the movie *Fatal Attraction*, Alex Forrest (Glen Close) says to Dan Gallagher (Michael Douglas), "You thought you could just walk into my life and turn it upside down without any thought for anyone but yourself." In fact, her behavior during the affair did just that to Dan, but she was a person without remorse or empathy for anyone else and could only see the events by the way she felt.

This was true for Gina as well. She had no empathy or concern for the wife. No one had ever shown Gina empathy as a child, so she never knew how to show it to anyone else. Gina's overriding need was to distract herself from the feelings within. Most of her affairs were short-lived because her lovers could not tolerate her neediness for long.

Gina became attached to many men and wanted them to marry her, but her demand for constant attention and reassurances, along with her clinginess, usually became a burden in a relationship. In fact, in *The Sopranos*, Gloria, referred to earlier as being drawn to Tony Soprano, the powerful man, was just such an individual. Her clinging and demanding behavior precipitated the end of the affair.

Gina couldn't understand why marriage eluded her. It was as though she lived her life stuck in a revolving door, repeating the same behavior. When some relationships lasted longer than others, Gina thought she was on her way to the altar, but she never got there. There are women like Gina, who *do* get to wear that coveted white wedding dress, but the basic problem remains and may begin to affect the marriage.

Childhood Sexual Abuse

Sharon is a twenty-eight-year-old medical technologist who has had many love affairs. Following is her story, as it was slowly revealed to me in therapy over time.

"The three of us—my mom, dad, and I—appeared to others as a close family. We attended church together on Sundays and sometimes went to community events in our small rural town. My mother was quiet and sweet. I felt sorry for her because she limped due to a congenital hip problem and often suffered from back pain because of it.

"I tried to be as helpful to her as I possibly could. I had to come right home from school and couldn't stay after class for club activities. If I had, I would have missed the bus, and Mom didn't drive.

"My dad managed a store in the nearby city, which was about a twenty-minute drive from our house. He was a lot of fun. He played the piano, and I would sing and dance. My mother sat on the sofa and watched, and clapped when we finished each song and I took my bows.

"But we were not a normal family, because my father sexually abused me from the time I was seven until I was twelve. His attention to me started early. At bedtime, he tucked me in and gave me a 'relaxing massage.' I remember once when I was a little girl and got sick during the night with a fever, he came in when he heard me crying. I saw that his pajamas had opened at the crotch. When he saw me staring, he smiled and hugged me tight. After that, I remember that on nights that he came home after working late, he came to my room in his pajamas and they were always open at the crotch, and I always looked.

"I realized later that he was like a lover, going from step to step, caressing me, kissing me sensually, and when I was twelve, his actions intensified, but did not go on for too long.

"All of my feelings were confused. I felt that something was wrong with what he was doing. It was very secretive and he told me I must never tell anyone or we couldn't continue to have our special time, and that if I did, he might have to move away. Although it made me uncomfortable, I felt excited by his massages and attention. I felt loved, and my body felt wonderful from his touch.

"When I was twelve, something else happened. My father was killed in a car accident coming home from work on one of his late nights. My grief seemed unbearable. Finally, my mother thought we should move because she was afraid to learn to drive, and it was impossible to keep up the house on her own. We moved to the nearby city where my father had worked and I made friends in our new neighborhood and seemed to have a more normal life.

"As I grew older, I realized what had happened to me at the hands of my father and that maybe this is why I seem to be attracted to married men."

Some women who have been sexually abused as children become sexually repressed as adults, but others like Sharon learned to associate sex with being "special" and they continue having one lover after another. They often come for therapy when their life is not going well and they can begin to understand how their current problems are related to the abuse of childhood.

Sharon's sexual behavior was an attempt to re-create the special feelings she had as a child, although probably not consciously, even though she understood the inappropriateness of her father's behavior. She has not been able to trust any of the men with whom she has had affairs, nor has she been able to find and maintain a mature relationship with a man. Without trust, a person cannot achieve the intimacy that is so vital to a mature relationship.

Searching for Parental Love

There are affairs that result from an individual's reaction to an absent or rejecting parent. The need for nurturing and a relationship with a parent when it is missing in childhood is a deprivation that continues to affect a person throughout life. It is important to have the support that comes from knowing there is someone there for you who loves you unconditionally. When it is missing, life can be a never-ending search for the mommy or daddy that the child wanted and needed.

A search for the unavailable lover can also be the result of competition with Mom for Dad's affection stemming from childhood experience. So the prize is winning out over Mother, only it is set later in the context of an affair. The victory is over the lover's wife who becomes a stand-in for Mother.

Not all adults will have affairs because of the search in one way or another for that love; some will deal with it in different ways.

Opportunity Near or Far

Geographical separation or geographical proximity can place a strain on individuals and their marriages. Being too close or too far can set the stage for affairs when a need is present.

Miles Apart

Carly e-mailed her husband, Joel, about how hard her day had been. She was on an anthropology dig in Israel, thousands of miles from home. It had been months since they had seen each other, and it became an effort to write the e-mails. Nothing unusual had happened because her job was routine—important, but routine.

She turned off her computer, brushed her hair, checked herself in the mirror, and left her compound to meet Samuel. He, too, was a senior scientist on the project. He was only a few months from retirement.

They were having a love affair.

He was older, wiser, and more "together" than anyone she had ever known. Their time together was wonderful. Carly dreaded their imminent separation, both by his retirement and her return home. She wanted to sort things out before this happened and didn't want them to each go their own way. But things didn't happen as Carly expected.

They were discovered. Samuel told her that they needed to end the affair. He told her he accepted full responsibility and that he was sick about the embarrassment it had caused them.

"It's the separation from home and family that brings something like this about. Ours is not the first and it won't be the last."

For Carly, the separation was traumatic because of abandonment issues in her childhood. She had to tell her husband, Joel, that she had been having an affair and he did not take it lightly. That is when they both entered marriage counseling.

Yet, affairs can happen even when the couple is together, rather than being geographically apart.

Attraction at Close Range

Paradoxically, affairs can happen when there is not a separation, but when people find themselves living and working closely together. This type of affair happens frequently and causes a tidal wave of problems when the other woman has a special relationship to the wife. It can be very toxic. Sometimes a sister or a sister-in-law can be involved with another family member. The enormity of affairs within the family can be felt for generations. A divorce does not always wipe the slate clean of repercussions.

The wife sustains a double wound, because those she thought had her best interests at heart have betrayed her trust. One such triangle, which occurs frequently, involves the best friend.

Ellen is Lola's best friend and she had an affair with Lola's husband, Jim. Ellen believes it happened slowly over time, and that Lola's actions set the stage for it to occur.

Lola had a high-powered position in a national public relations firm based in Washington, D.C. She had met Ellen at a spa at lunchtime, and they began a friendship that became very close. In Ellen's words:

> "We spent a lot of time together. We really were like sisters. We bought each other gifts. Lola's gifts to me were very expensive, more than I could ever spend on her. She had a top-management job and could afford it. There were many perks for her, like tickets to shows and events, and she often took both Jim and me. When Lola couldn't go, I went with Jim.
>
> "After a while, the three of us spent more time together. We went to dinner, art fairs, all sorts of events. I was often included in their evenings out.

"Jim was very handsome, but more than that, he was delightful to be with. He smiled, joked, and was so friendly and gregarious that people he didn't know always seemed to stop and chat with him.

"The turning point came when Lola's job became more demanding and she had to work even longer hours. She and Jim had tickets for the symphony, the theater, and basketball games. Whenever she found that she had to work, she gave me her ticket, and I went with Jim. Two things happened. Lola became very stressed from changes at work, and very short-tempered. The other thing was that I became very attracted to Jim. At first, it was uncomfortable for me when I found myself going to concerts with him, but gradually I began looking forward to it, and even hoping Lola had to work.

"Jim and I became lovers. I was never so happy. I never really had a serious relationship. I know I am overweight and most guys are not attracted to me. Lola was very beautiful and dynamic. But I knew in my heart he didn't love me. He was reacting to Lola's change.

"Lola found out about us, and went into a rage. She wrote me a long, angry letter about my betrayal. Jim never called me again. Lola stopped coming to the spa at lunchtime.

"I tried calling, but they had changed their phone number to an unlisted one. Jim wouldn't take my calls at work. I wrote to him, but the letters were returned unopened. A few months later, I wrote again, and the return letter was stamped "not at this address." I called Lola at work, and found she no longer worked there.

"They have disappeared from my life. I feel a great loss."

People in close proximity, whether through work, friendship, family, or being neighbors, can come to know each other intimately. Such closeness without regard to boundaries places the relationship at high risk for developing into a sexual affair.

Transitional Issues

As we know, individuals go through life stages and many periods of transition—when they leave home, graduate high school or college, are engaged, married, have children, retire, and grow older. Any transition can cause us to be anxious. This is true even though the transition may be a happy one that we are looking forward to. The anxiety arises because we are assuming a new role, responsibilities, and challenges.

Dr. Nancy Schlossberg, adult developmental psychologist, has defined "transitions" in a way that takes this into account. In her article "A Model for Analyzing Human Adaptation to Transition," published in *The Counseling Psychologist,* she says that "a transition is an event or nonevent resulting in a change in assumptions about oneself and the world." We understand that the obvious transitions can cause stress because of the uncertainty that change brings. But transitions also occur when some of these events *don't* happen. We must adjust to the non-event because the way we look at ourselves will be different. If the marriage doesn't occur or the baby is not conceived or the position is not offered, a transition has occurred because you must think of yourself in a different way.

Transitions also occur with unexpected events, like being fired from a job where you are feeling quite secure, or the death of a child. These events change your life and cause stress. When we are stressed, we are more vulnerable and emotionally reactive. We may not have the capacity to work through the anxiety as safely as we would like.

Individual Life Transitions

Jackie's story is one of a transition due to a nonevent, even though she had assumed that it would occur.

"Most of all, I want to be married and have kids. I did everything to meet Mr. Right. After finishing graduate school, I realized there were fewer opportunities to meet men. I did what other women were doing at the time—I answered personal ads, went to bars, then chat rooms and matchmakers online. Finally, I went to expensive matchmakers offline. When this didn't work, I gave up and stopped trying. I accepted the fact that I would probably not get married and definitely would not be a mom. Then I met Bill at a professional meeting. I saw his wedding ring. I knew he was married. But he was fun and attractive, and we became lovers.

"My life with him is limited, but the time we have together is quality time. What do I want? I want the life his wife has."

Jackie's nonevent—not getting married—caused her anxiety and unhappiness. Individuals can run into difficulties down the path of life that need attention. If corrections are not made, the problem can get worse or the individual tries to reduce anxiety in another way. Sometimes it is overinvolvement in work, sometimes alcoholism, drugs, gambling—and sometimes an affair. A woman can meet a man who is trying to resolve some personal issue through an affair, or she herself will seek the solution through an affair.

Family Stages and Transitions

Families, like individuals, have stages. Each stage is really a transition that can cause stress as the family tries to adjust to it. It may be the arrival of the first child or the launching of the last one into the world. With transitions, our world changes and we need to integrate this into our lives. This requires skills. When the change does not go smoothly, it may cause dissatisfaction. Rather than working through the problems, one of the pair may have an affair. Sometimes, it is the wife who will go looking for someone else, or she may become receptive to another man's advances.

There are times when sexual desire diminishes or a couple feels dissatisfaction with their sexual life. At times, it can be due to the stress and pressures of family and/or professional life. Sometimes, it is due to the unrealistic expectations of what a marriage is and what it can provide. In all relationships, the initial passion will decrease and one can think one has fallen out of love. Such thoughts are upsetting to the individual. At such times, a wife or husband may be more receptive to an affair with its excitement, high levels of passion, and increased self-esteem.

The following statements indicate the stress that can accompany life stages and transitions:

"I'm going to be thirty-eight next month and I want Lloyd to leave Sara and marry me. I want to have children and time is not on my side."

"I don't know why I spent so much time preparing for this career. It's a disappointment. Something is missing in my life."

"I am so bored. Bob and I don't seem to have much to say to each other. The house is so quiet. Ben, our youngest, has gone off to college. The people I meet online have much more interest in me than Bob does."

"Charles resents my involvement in work. He wants us to start a family. How can I? I don't have time for pregnancy and he just won't understand this."

"I feel so alone since John died. I can't believe it. I thought we would grow old together, not that he would die right before his fiftieth birthday. Three years later and I find the loneliness overwhelming. I'm too young for this. Single men are not interested in someone my age."

"I just feel unhappy and I don't know why."

The stage is set for an affair in all these situations. These women's statements indicate a problem that may only need venting and good communication skills to resolve, but on a closer look may be real despair. The point is to take that closer look.

Your lover's reasons for the affair are as important to understand as yours are. A man going through a transition that hits him hard can attempt to deal with his pain by having an affair. If you are there at the time this is occurring, you may become romantically involved with him. This can happen at any age. This is illustrated in the delightful film *Moonstruck*. Cosmo Castorini (played by Vincent Gardenia) is an older man having an affair with a younger woman. Rose (Olympia Dukakis), his wife, confronts him about his infidelity and tells him that he is growing old and will die anyhow—affair or no affair. He finally understands, and gives up the affair.

Many affairs occur between the older married man and the younger woman. And the affair may be exactly what Rose in *Moonstruck* deduces: a reaction to aging, which is a difficult life transition for some. The reverse is also true—many women are having affairs with married men younger than themselves.

The Chronic Hassle

Another variation of Dr. Schlossberg's work on transitions is what she has coined "the chronic hassle," which refers to an ongoing problem that an individual or a couple might have as part of their everyday life. Because these problems are serious, unrelenting, and constant, they may change the way a person views himself and the world and, thus, by definition are a transition.

I have often been told stories by both men and women of challenges they face from the time they open their eyes in the morning until they close them again at night, only to wake up the next day to the same situation. Many such unrelenting challenges are related to health, poverty, raising a chronically ill child, coping with a severely alcoholic spouse, dealing with a teenage child with a drug problem, living with a mentally ill family member, or long-term unemployment.

Clients have told me that their chronic hassles create anxiety so uncomfortable that it cries out for relief. Sometimes the relief takes the form of an affair.

Leslie is a thirty-two-year-old mother of two very young girls who have a serious genetic disease. This illness requires constant attention and will most likely take the girls' lives before they reach adulthood. Leslie is involved with a married man who has a child with the same illness. They met while attending a support group for parents.

Leslie tearfully told me, "I love him. Without him, how could I get up in the morning? I can't tell you how hard it is to look at your children and know their future is so bleak. He and I have so much in common. His wife is cold. She won't come to the support-group meetings. He loves me, but doesn't think he should leave her with the burden. In a way I know what that means because my husband leaves the whole job to me."

The positive feelings that result from the affair are in and of themselves reinforcing. The cause of the chronic hassle remains, but the escape into the affair is something they look forward to. The affair can become intense, as it did for Leslie.

Life is a series of transitions and it is at such times that people who are vulnerable may look for comfort in someone's arms. At such a moment, a woman may find she is involved with a married man, primarily because he is having trouble negotiating his own life transition. Or the reverse may be true—that she is the one in turmoil.

If you are that person, the question is, will you find that comfort for whatever reason you are having the affair? Or will the affair bring more anxiety to your life?

That is one of the questions we will continue to explore together in this book.

Part II

The Marital Triangle

Chapter Three

About Her

*Y*ou may be a complete stranger to his wife. Or, she may suspect you exist, or she may know who you are. She may have hired a private investigator to confirm her suspicions, or even have followed him herself and discovered your identity. Or, she may suspect your existence, but then has doubts or doesn't really want to know you exist. This state of confusion was described by Joyce Carol Oates in her novel, *The Falls*, about Ariah's husband's affair, "Ariah knew, but didn't know. As a wife doesn't know, yet knows. Or believes she knows."

Or you may have some connection to her. You may have met her at an office Christmas party or you may even have been to their home. As a friend, you may have visited them, you could work with her, be a neighbor, or even her best friend. If she finds out who you are, she will be angry. And if she knows you, either she may have suspected or be surprised. Either way, she will see your affair with her husband as a double betrayal. In Sabina's case, she knew her husband's lover:

> "I can't believe it was April. She works with him and has been to our house. She knows our children. I am angry at her, but just as angry at his secretary, Lee, for arranging the meetings and calling me with his excuses. All the while laughing up her sleeve at me. Now, when Lee calls, she's as sweet as pie, but she doesn't fool me. I have a long memory."

If your lover's wife learns about you, after the initial shock, she'll be the one searching for information. She may ask some of the following questions.

Do you love her?
Do you want to marry her?
Who else knows?
Is it over?
What is she like in bed?
What does she look like?
How did you meet?
How does she dress?
What did she wear when you first met?

If she knows about you, she is jealous. And you, of course, likely feel the same about her. You want to be with him on his birthday, Christmas, and Valentine's Day, but that is impossible. You will get a card, a gift, a phone call, or a substitute celebration at a later time. She will get the real thing, as well as his company. You may obsess over what they are doing together on these occasions, as well as wonder what she is like.

> *Candice:* "Holidays are bad. I feel very sad. I guess I feel rejected. Members of my support group get together. It helps to take my mind off him being with her. I really hate this part of it."

What Is She Like?

Regardless of whether or not you know her, you may be very interested in his wife. She is your competition and you believe she stands in the way of your happiness. If she were not there, you believe he would be free to marry you. You are often very jealous of her. You may be aware of her schedule, and you may resent her lifestyle. You certainly resent the attention he pays her. As Diane put it, "She's living the life I want."

Much of your information comes from her husband. He may complain that she spends too much on clothes or nags him about not spending enough time at home. Husbands run the gamut; he may talk about how horrible his wife is and how bad their marriage is, or he may compartmentalize his two worlds so that you hear nothing about her. He may not even mention her name. You may do the same. Even though you may want to know as much as you can about her to learn what the competition is like, you may not mention her, in an effort to avoid the reality of her existence.

What He Tells You

If he talks about her, you may have no way of knowing the truth about the information he gives you. Although you want to believe the negative comments, because you believe it strengthens the chance of him leaving her to marry you. You believe it, despite the fact that they may have been married for many years. If you know her, you may have formed your own opinion, and sometimes his version may not fit with what you believe.

Helen's experience reflects just this type of incongruity:

"I don't know what to think. I see her at work and she doesn't seem to be the ogre that Steve describes."

Maybe Steve is telling Helen what he wants her to know, not the reality of his life at home. Why would he do that? When you think that things are really bad in their marriage, it gives you hope to think that the situation is so terrible at home that there is a good possibility he will leave her. It is to his advantage that you think their life together is problematic. It gives you hope and ensures you will continue trying to please him. You try harder to make those times when he is away from her as wonderful as you can, to be as beautiful as possible, and to keep him from harboring any concerns about your relationship. If he indicates that everything is great at home yet is still having an affair with you, chances are you would think he's a cad.

Jill: "I don't think I have ever met anyone sweeter. I treasure our time together and try to make it perfect. I feel I don't have the amount of time she has with him, but I can make it up with the quality of time we have together. And I do that. I plan it as perfectly as I can. I am conscious of creating memories—good ones."

When you hear of the many complaints he has about her, you may find yourself trying to be just the opposite of her, fearful of exhibiting any of the terrible traits he speaks of. This may be very difficult because some of what he describes may really be her response to his behavior. And when he exhibits the same behavior with you, you find yourself actually responding or wanting to respond in the same way his wife does. You almost understand her at that point.

> *Jan:* "He is so disorganized, he's driving me crazy. I bought him a Day Runner for Christmas. I had it monogrammed. I would love to have put an inscription on it, but I wouldn't dare. Sometimes he forgets his Day Runner or leaves it here. When you are having an affair you have to be organized!"

According to him, his wife causes him such difficulties that you find yourself being the counselor, trying to help him with his life at home. You feel that he needs understanding. He complains that she doesn't understand. So you try your best to do just that. If you are married, you probably join with him in sharing the unhappiness you feel about your own marriage. You become a support system for each other with the issues he has with her, and you with your husband. While the emotional support this offers is comforting, it avoids the underlying issues that may well have led both of you to the affair.

After some soul-searching, Dee came to understand that maybe she and Brad were drawn together for other reasons and it would be best if she could understand what they were:

> "I was so much in love with him that I was consumed with thinking about him, but there was something in the back of my mind telling me that something isn't really right here. We both have all these complaints about our spouses. I decided to seek therapy to try to figure it out. After a few sessions I knew I had to stop seeing Brad until I better understood myself. And to know why I am finding such discontent in my life. It is very hard because he keeps calling, and sometimes I go and sometimes I don't. I know that sends mixed messages. But I don't want to jump out of the frying pan into the fire."

Dee is right to try to understand the problems in her marriage and to get to the source, since the divorce rate is higher for second marriages than for first ones. She knows she can't judge their relationship on the basis of the thrill of an affair. The excitement and the rise in self-esteem that result from an affair can obliterate the reasons she is having an affair. It would be wise for Brad to do the same. There could be any number of reasons for Brad's dissatisfaction with his life. For example, Brad and his wife may be experiencing a difficult life transition, or they may have unrealistic expectations of each other, or one or the other could be carrying over some emotional issues from childhood that need to be resolved. So Dee is right in thinking that she could be jumping into the fire.

What He Doesn't Tell You

On the other hand, if he compartmentalizes his two lives, he tells you little about her. So you wonder what she is like and you feel that you have little information to gauge the course of your relationship. Your mind works overtime looking for clues.

> *Marti:* "I ask questions about her in what I think is a subtle way, but he ignores them, distracts me with kisses or tells me that he is here with me and that's what counts. But I worry about why he doesn't talk to me about her."

You may even wonder if she is a perfectly lovely person and your lover is having the affair for other reasons than his difficulties with her. Some of the reasons men enter affairs are the same as those of women we discussed earlier, but there are some additional reasons.

If you are the type of woman who wants to know about his wife and he rarely mentions her, you may spend considerable time wondering what exactly it is *about her* that led him to the affair—to validate your belief that it *is* her fault.

Is It Her?

It is common wisdom that the affair is the wife's fault. Everyone knows she is a failure as a wife if he has to look elsewhere. Maybe she's not good enough in bed or more than likely she just doesn't understand him. He is usually without fault. You probably wonder if perhaps she *isn't* the cause of his having the affair. Maybe she is attractive, interesting, and sexy, so why is he having an affair with me? Is it because he has fallen out of love with her and in love with me?

For everyone involved, it is important to know why he is having the affair, just as it is important for you to know why you are involved with him.

She Is No Longer Desirable

You need to understand his wife and her background. She may be very sexy and make him very happy in bed. Reports indicate that the husband is not necessarily looking for better sex. It might be great at home, and it isn't the sex with you that necessarily attracts him. She may be even more attractive than you!

> *Clarice:* "I knew he was having an affair and I finally caught him at it. I followed him when he went into her apartment and then came out with her. I didn't make a scene because I was stunned that she was a regular-looking person, not what I had imagined. She wasn't bad looking—she just wasn't what I expected. When I confronted him, he couldn't even give me a reason, beyond that it was exciting. It's hard for a marriage to keep up with excitement. I told him, 'You want excitement, I'll give you excitement!' and the color drained from his face."

In fact, as a therapist who has sat with many couples helping to resolve their issues of infidelity, I will tell you most of the wives were attractive, charming, and delightful. I have found the second woman in the triangle sometimes to be the same, but not always.

So, is it her?

She Doesn't Understand Him

It's not beauty and sex that are the real draw. So could it be that his "she doesn't understand me" excuse may also not be true? After years of living with him, his wife may understand him better than anyone. And that may be the problem. Maybe she understands him and just doesn't like what she sees. Remember, she sees him in the real world. She knows how he treats others, if he is fair, kind, or if he is disrespectful to women, children, and the elderly. She knows how he treats his parents, his siblings and coworkers. She knows how he handles anger, a crisis, a misunderstanding. So the possibility exists that she does understand him. In fact, she may be an authority on him. So, is it her?

She's a Nag

Is she a nag? Maybe. Or could she be frustrated over issues they have between them or individually that haven't been resolved and are affecting their relationship? The significant issue is how this person feels about himself. How does the affair meet his needs? He may be expecting his wife to satisfy his emotional or psychological issues that she cannot, and most likely you cannot either. These needs may have nothing to do with the women in his life, but may have everything to do with him, and may have been there long before he met either of you. One consideration is that an affair can be a distraction from solving individual problems. Psychiatrist Frank Pittman writes, in *Man Enough*, "The roots of infidelity are in the defective relationship between a man and his father, not a defective marriage." You must consider that it may not be her. He may have looked to his marriage or to her to solve these problems or to make him feel better about himself. If she can't accomplish this, he may be looking toward you and the affair for the solution. She is not the bad wife if she cannot do that for him. He must meet this challenge himself. If he is a poor-risk partner, more than likely she has serious issues with him. So, is it her?

A Romantic Retreat

She cannot provide the welcome retreat for him that an affair provides. She, like most wives, must cope with the two most hectic times of day for a family: they are at the beginning and end of the day. If there are children, she must prepare each family member for the day. She may be irritable and preoccupied in the hectic environment, with breakfast and lunches to make, kids to supervise, carpools to drive, problems to solve in getting everyone launched for the day. A similar scenario happens at the end of the day when everyone comes home tired and hungry, and there is much for her to do before settling down for the evening. She must attend to or supervise dinner, baths, homework, and many household chores may occupy that time. Even if there are no children, these times of the day can be hectic. It is a time when she would like to come home from work, "kick back," and have a glass of wine with him and talk over the day, but it is not possible because she is on her second shift. With you, however, he can have that glass of wine and talk.

Contrast this with the calm and serene time he spends with you. You go out for dinner, or call for take-out, or one of you may cook. No one is harried. There may be soft lights, quiet music, and time to focus on each other. It is fun, secretive, and romantic, and it is unlikely that a child will throw a hairbrush down the toilet and you'll have to deal with a plunger and dirty water all over the floor. The most that is required of him is to use the corkscrew to open the bottle of wine.

So the affair may have little to do with her. Her worst crime is attending to her duties. So, is it her?

Relationship Stages

It may not be her at all, but their stage of marriage. Most likely, their marriage is not in the early stage where passion is high, but your relationship is. The affair with you gives him the sexual high that he loved so much from the early years of his marriage. As a marriage progresses, it passes the initial infatuation phase. At this point, some people feel, as previously noted, they have fallen out of love and do not realize that their marriage is going through one of its many stages. The character of love changes through the years. He wants the passion stage back. The secrecy and special feeling of being just the two of you is something that is hard for her to create and a situation she cannot compete with unless they were to recognize the impact of family life and the stages of marriage on their lives and work at a solution together. They would find that there are ways to bring excitement and renewal into their marriage.

This issue must be balanced against the longevity of their marriage and the intimacy they have built. Because passion will begin to decline in relationships, you could find yourself in the same position she is in now at some point in the future. So, is it her?

Gender Differences

Sometimes, men have affairs because they look at relationships differently than women do. Most women have affairs not primarily for sex, as people believe men do, but for other reasons. Women feel they need to love the man or have very special feelings for him. You seldom hear a man say he couldn't have sex with her because he equated sex with love, as women say. He doesn't feel that way. Although it appears to be very macho to have an affair, the affair is not as much about the woman as it is about satisfying his emotional needs. Most women are interested in intimacy, which is why so many affairs are off balance, with the man having a *fling* and the woman having a *romantic love affair*. This means that you and the wife have the same goal of wanting him in a permanent relationship.

In *Sex in America: A Definitive Survey*, Robert T. Michael et al. present their findings on adult sexual behavior based on intensive interviews with 3,432 adults between eighteen and fifty-nine. On the issue of gender differences, they write, "Many more women than men are looking for love and consider marriage to be a prerequisite for sex. . . . Many more men than women are looking for sexual play and pleasure, with marriage or even love not necessarily part of it."

No one causes another person to have an affair. He is having the affair because he chooses to have it, even if his sex life at home needs a tune-up or his wife nags or doesn't understand him— or even if their sex life *doesn't* need a tune-up, she *doesn't* nag, and she *does* understand him. This is important information for you to understand. First, she may be the opposite of what he tells you, and second, his affair has more to do with him emotionally, than with her or you. Additionally, there are other remedies for their problems than his affair. What is crucial for you to know is if your affair is more important to him than his marriage. You also need information about her to help you figure out if he will leave her for you.

Information You Need to Know

Information is power. The more you know about her, him, and about yourself, the easier it will be to find the answer to your question: Will he really leave her to marry me? There are red flags that you can spot and that warn you your attention is needed.

Infidelity in Her Family

Family information, especially on infidelity, for everyone in the marital triangle is another helpful piece in this puzzle. Affairs can often be seen throughout generations of a family. For many families, it becomes a way to handle stress or shows a pattern of behavior. If the wife's family has a history of infidelity, then the way in which other members of the family respond to its discovery will give you more information on what she is likely to do. If the women in the family look away, do not confront it, and accept it, that may help you in finding the answer to your question.

For example, the family of President John F. Kennedy had generations of infidelity that was accepted by nearly all the women in the family. It was not condoned—they chose to look the other way.

It may be hard for you to know her family's information, unless it is shared with you. If it should be shared, you will see the reactions of the women in her family to their husband's infidelity and you will have more information on what you can expect. It is because family information is so important that family therapists want to know the *generational* history. You will see this discussed more in depth later in the book.

Where Does Her Power Come From?

The wife is in a position of power, even though most are too fragile at the time of discovery of an affair to realize that. Her power comes from several sources. The major source is their history together. If they have been together for a significant period of time, they have much emotional investment in each other from the ups and downs of life that they have lived through together—the children they conceived, raised, enjoyed and worried over, the adversities they have overcome, and the joys they have shared. They have families that have shared in all of this, as well as friends. They have accumulated memories, some from great experiences they have had together and others from living through hardships. It may be hard for you to believe because of the stories he tells you about her. The bottom line is they have developed an attachment that may be difficult for him to break and to even realize exists until he contemplates leaving her.

His Fear the Affair Will Become Public

Many men do not want their children, parents, in-laws, or friends to know about their infidelity. If it is a work affair, it could be disastrous for his career if it comes out. His wife understands this, and she has power in this situation. She can threaten to make it public or to tell someone else whose opinion is important to him. It is my observation that the wife will fight to keep her husband and protect her children and may make the threat and follow through if it is not effective.

Charlene is a case in point. When she realized her husband, Scott, a pediatrician, was having an affair with the mother of one of his patients, Charlene tearfully confronted him. He apologized and promised to end it, but she soon discovered he hadn't. She went to the owner of the practice and told him. When the owner became concerned that Scott's affair would affect the practice he had so carefully nurtured and built over the years, he asked Scott to find another place to practice within the year.

His Comfort in His Marriage

The reasons he gives you that prevent him from leaving at that time, and the future dates you must wait for, are either signs that he is more comfortable than you think in his marriage and these are tactics to put you off, or they are signs of his ambivalence. In the former case, there is little hope that he will leave; in the latter, there is more hope, because it may show ambivalence. It may be that he is working through a process. She has the most power when he feels remorse and believes he has made a mistake.

Children and Family

Their children and their families are important sources of power for his wife. Most men care very much about what their children will think, and this becomes a deterrent for some, if not a stumbling block. Many men I have counseled have been very ashamed of facing their in-laws about their affair. One man told me in tears that his father-in-law said, "Now I, too, can't trust you. I feel betrayed. I gave my daughter's life over to you and you failed us."

Others say the in-laws say nothing, but they recognize a difference in how they relate to them.

> "It's been two years and there is this uncomfortable reserve between us that was never there before. I know they can't forgive me or forget how I hurt their daughter. I've been a disappointment."

I have helped many men prepare for talks with their wife's family and listened to letters of apology to her parents. Many have had to address the issue with their own parents and felt ashamed. This is a source of power for the wife.

Their Financial Situation

The financial issue is a major one for many couples. I have seen many people decide to stay in a marriage they would like to leave because of money. Before women advanced in business, academia, and government, they were concerned about how they would make it on their own if their marriage should dissolve. To some extent these advances have reduced their fears, but only slightly. The man may also be worried about how he will be able live without a two-couple income. The wife has the same concerns. Unless he has considerable wealth, both their lifestyles may change significantly.

The married couple also may have worked out a beneficial financial situation that depends on their being together. Dramatic changes in their lifestyle may occur with a divorce. These changes may become a serious barrier for him to consider, but they also become leverage for the wife. They may agree that it is best to stay married. For some, it is the impetus to work harder on the marriage. In the TV series *The Sopranos*, even wealthy Tony complains about the finances and the lifestyle changes their separation and possible divorce is causing him. This, of course, increases her power.

There are some additional complications that work in his wife's favor and increase her power. He may be involved in her family's business or her father may have been instrumental in his professional advancement. He may feel indebted to her parents for financial assistance with loans, down payments for their home, or for help with college expenses.

Her Support System

Women often have support from family and friends. They are also more likely to find support from a therapist or a women's group. Such care helps sustain her. Support is powerful and almost a necessity.

There are other types of support besides emotional. Many women see a lawyer, not for divorce, but to know their rights and what they can expect if they proceed with one. They also consult with an accountant and financial planner because they feel their marriage is now like a house of cards. It may all fall apart, leaving them with nothing. They no longer trust him and when they recover from the initial shock, many believe they must start to look after themselves in case their marriage ends.

> *Rachel:* "Look, he spent lots of our savings on her. I need to protect myself and I will do whatever it takes. He is furious at me for some of the financial changes I have made. I didn't make them in a vacuum. I just got scared. I'm 53 and I can't start over very easily. I must take care of myself if I am looking at a future without him."

His Work

Depending on his professional situation, his wife may have considerable power. If having an affair will cause him excessive embarrassment or loss of confidence by clients, customers, or colleagues, she may have power. The world is changing in many respects, but polls continue to show that the American public still frowns upon extramarital affairs. In the survey presented in *Sex in America: A Definitive Survey*, 76.7 percent of the survey group agreed with the statement: "Extramarital sex is always wrong."

Infidelity can affect a man's career. Harry C. Stonecipher, a Boeing executive, was forced to resign after the company discovered he was having an affair with Debra Peabody, a vice president in the Washington office. After working for Boeing for twenty years, Mr. Stonecipher was also forced to forfeit his employment benefits as a result of the affair, according to the *New York Times* (19 March 2005). Now, all Boeing employees must sign a code of ethical conduct. It will be interesting to see if this becomes the new test for executives. Would your lover sign it?

A Fragile Wife

Some husbands think twice about leaving a wife who is seriously ill or who has suffered a severe loss. If she has had a history of suicide attempts or intractable depression, he may fear she would be unable to withstand the pain of his leaving. Sometimes a family has a child with a chronic disabling illness who requires significant care. Because this type of power comes from unfortunate circumstances, it is hardly recognized as power. The wife doesn't have to use it as power, but his conscience may make it so. Whether or not she realizes her power, the wife is hit hard by his infidelity. She suffers both physically and emotionally. Many husbands are reluctant to inflict this pain on their wives.

After Discovery

The woman who has found out about her husband's affair is quite different after discovering the news than she was before, and usually her husband is different as well.

Her Reaction

She is devastated, shocked, and vacillates between rage and depression. She can't sleep and can't eat, or she can't stop eating or sleeping excessively. It is not uncommon to see a woman lose forty pounds in a short period of time. She obsesses about the affair and bombards him with questions during the day and often through the night. She no longer trusts him and wants him to account for his time to be sure he is not seeing you.

> *Ruth:* "When I found out about the affair, I wondered what did I do wrong. What could I change? I wanted a makeover. I tried soft music at dinner. How could that work with little kids? Then I got angry. He had no right to put me in that situation. He's a father. He knows what goes on in a family."

Ruth is like most women after the discovery of an affair. She assumes responsibility for his behavior. She felt guilt and tried to make changes, but the affair had nothing to do with her. It had everything to do with a husband who emotionally and sexually abandoned her because he wasn't mature enough to cope with adult responsibilities. No marriage can sustain the high levels of passion seen in the early stages of a romance. The marriage will change and it will grow in depth as it matures. The growing pains will always be there, but so will the joys.

> *Tracy:* "I can't be 'put together' when he comes home. I've been teaching school, running errands, driving carpools. I can't measure up to his girlfriend. How can I?"

> *Dottie:* "I don't know how he could do this to us. Father's Day is next week. Some father, huh? He's taken the joy out of our life."

He will hear these types of statements many times after the discovery. If it resonates with him and he feels guilt and remorse, that will support their staying together. If he shows no sympathy or remorse, the marriage is in trouble.

His Reaction

It is at this point that couples usually seek marital counseling. The reaction is so intense that many feel they cannot heal without help.

Healing infidelity is not an easy task and having an experienced professional help guide them through the process is a wise choice. He will be asked to give up his affair with you, to be monogamous, and to work on whatever issues there are that were influential in the development of the affair. There are a number of possible scenarios for how it will play out, and how he will react to the discovery of the affair.

Shock at her reaction

Often, men are truly shocked and bewildered by how hard the affair hits their wife, and sometimes it causes them to feel truly remorseful. Once again, it goes back to the gender differences. Most men see the affair in terms of sex and believe it has nothing to do with their marriage or their love for their wives. They are not as introspective as their wives and so do not look at underlying issues.

More women than I can count have told me that they would not have sex with a man unless they loved them or had very special feelings for them. Therefore, these women have a very difficult time believing that the affair had nothing to do with love. Because of this typically male belief, which runs counter to their own, women are devastated by the news of the affair. In view of his belief system about affairs, he is bewildered by her reaction.

Michael: "I'm shocked at how she took this."

Mark: "It didn't matter what I said. She wouldn't stop crying."

Frank: "It scared me. I didn't know what to do. I mean, I thought maybe I should call 911. It really felt like an emergency. It wasn't as calm as they portray it in the movies."

Larry: "I've never seen her this way. She's actually physically sick over this."

The husband sits opposite me in complete disbelief over his wife's reaction. He feels extreme remorse and guilt because he just cannot believe it could have affected her so badly. He would do anything to reverse his actions and to not have had the affair happen.

It means nothing to me

The phrase that I hear the most often from the husband—and that I hesitate to write because of the pain I know it will cause the reader—is, "It means nothing to me."

If the husband says that the affair means nothing to him, he will agree to stop his affair immediately and we will discuss together the best way to do this. If you are having the affair with a married man, then you can see how important it is to know the truth as early as you can. The man who is only having a fling is one who can so easily say, "She didn't mean anything to me."

I love her and I want to marry her

Another scenario is one in which the husband has fallen in love with his lover and he is in limbo between what he wants to do and what he feels he should do. Most men make a decision at this point. If he leaves, the wife stays in counseling to help her understand why this has happened and to help her cope with the painful aftermath.

Jeanine: "It is a big blow to think he would give it all up for another woman. We have kids and a life together. I never thought it would happen to me. The only comfort I take is that he cares enough to work in counseling to help me understand. I hate her, but basically I think she is lucky."

I love her, but it is over

If he gives up the affair with a woman he has fallen in love with he will then be grieving his loss. This period is very painful for him and for the wife who must bear witness to his pain. It is the same for his lover. It is particularly difficult for the lover if she is a married woman, because she must carry on as wife and mother and only give in to her grief when she is alone. Everyone in this triangle is experiencing a loss and grieving.

Nita: "I'm going out of my mind seeing the change in him. He's lost his joie de vivre. I pray daily for the strength to live through this. I believe we can get back to where we were. I believe it, because he is truly sorry and because we didn't have such a bad marriage. It was good. It could have been better, but it was good."

I am not ending this affair

The man who is experiencing this as a romantic love affair is the one who may leave his marriage. He is the one who will make the decision whether to stay in his marriage, leave, or just continue as is. The wife may look the other way and allow the affair to go on. She may at this point, or later, decide to divorce him. She has had it! She usually makes such a decision later in the process, when she is stronger emotionally, understands why the affair occurred, and has given up hope of him ending the affair.

> *Nancy:* "My head is clearer now and I know this is the best decision. But I still love him."

There is always the possibility that he will give up the affair when he sees she is serious about leaving him, but in my experience that is rare. If he does, it is because it suits his own purposes. Many men who have affairs and won't give them up and won't work on the marriage are narcissistic. This means they only care how the events affect them. Be warned: a narcissistic, self-centered husband is no bargain!

Issues for Her

She will be going through a very difficult period and will be coping with strong emotions, disappointment, and trying to resolve and integrate the affair into her life. Just as you have tried to understand what she is like and how she figures into your future, so she does the same about you. And just as you may have come to some erroneous conclusions, so may she have.

Jealousy

Both women in this triangle will feel jealousy and envy. You will probably envy her the position she has as wife with all of the rights and privileges that come with that. She will be jealous of you because you have been able to attract her husband. This makes her doubt herself in many ways. She has a severe drop in self-esteem. She will want to know about you, your personality, your figure, your age, your looks, and what special attraction you have that drew her husband to you.

If she knows you, she will be angrier than if she doesn't, but she will still want to know the answers to those questions. If you are her best friend, she will look at you differently and will obsessively review all your interactions, with her looking for the clues she missed.

> *Janice:* "When I think back on how I left them together and went to an outing with the kids, or how I was at work and they were having a 'roll in the hay,' I could scream! Why? She's pitiful. She's overweight. I don't get it."

She will also feel very jealous over the intimacy the two of you may have developed. She will want to know what you have shared about her. If he has shared personal information about their marriage, their sexual relationship, her weaknesses, or any other confidence, she will feel keenly betrayed.

Blame

There are wives who feel they can handle the situation better if you get all the blame or bear a considerable amount of it. My experience has been that most often the wife holds both of you to blame, but for many women it is easier to live with him and continue in the marriage if she feels it is your fault. She might believe you lured him with sex. She may think that she fails in comparison to your beauty and sex appeal, but she has no respect for you. On the other hand, she may not be able to understand it, because you are not that beautiful.

> *Ellen:* "I don't understand his choice. She's older than he is. Who ever heard of that, having an affair with someone older? He's like Prince Charles, cheating on Diana for that Camilla woman and then marrying her. Personally, I think it sucks!"

She believes you are trying to rob her of all that she holds dear and that you have soiled something sacred. She feels you have cheated her of memories.

Diane: "Bob and I used to go to New York for Valentine's Day. It was our tradition. We stayed at the Ritz-Carlton and had room service and we took in a ballet, a few shows, and the museums. He always bought me a sexy gown or some underwear. This year I was very disappointed that he had to be away on business. I found out he did all that with her. Took her to the Ritz-Carlton. I couldn't believe it! Deep down I believe he was doing that to be sadistic because he knew someday I would find out. But, you see, he wrecked a memory and if we continue together we can never go there again."

Should the Women Meet?

At different times, one of the women wants to meet the other, out of curiosity or out of a desire to impart some caustic information to the other.

Diane: "I just wanted to tell her that she doesn't appreciate him and I do. She doesn't deserve a husband like that."

Cindy: "I wanted to kill her. I wanted to ask her what right she had to try to break up a family. There's more to life than sex."

An angry confrontation will not resolve the problem. It may give some satisfaction for a few moments because you have released a pressure valve, but this is only temporary. As a general rule, meeting and screaming at each other is not a good idea.

Money Spent on the Affair

It costs money to have an affair. Instead of going out a lot, you try to get out of town because it reduces the chance of getting caught. You receive gifts from him and often some financial help as you get to know each other better. That money comes from their family funds and she will be very angry about it. She will remember her sacrifices and your fun.

Justine: "I came upon a receipt in the wastebasket. It caught my attention with all of this focus on identity theft. It was all scrunched up and I opened it and saw it was a receipt for a cashmere sweater from an upscale store on El Paseo Drive. It had to be a gift for me for my birthday in three weeks. I suppose that's why he used cash so I wouldn't see it on the charge. I don't usually stand on ceremony. I start talking about my birthday in advance and make comments about what I'd like to do, but this year I didn't have to because I thought he was taking care of it. I was very excited, but my birthday came and went and he didn't even remember, and he didn't give me the cashmere sweater. Well, we had a big fight and now I know. He was screwing around with someone he met online. I am devastated."

As time passed and the initial shock dissipated, Justine came back to the subject of the cashmere sweater.

"He cheated me of my expectations of my marriage. I feel tainted by the thought of them having sex. Then I think of our money that he spent on her, and I feel despair. I am very careful about spending money. There are things we want and I don't buy them. What right did he have to deprive our kids of something, just for his affair?"

Obsession

The wife feels plagued by a continual mental review of what she imagines this affair to be like. But more than that, she reviews their past interactions looking for clues to see how this developed and why she knew nothing about it.

Justine: "I can't sleep. I keep going over the conversation we had, I mean the fight, on my birthday. I think of how they could have been meeting. I remember he had a lot of business calls on his cell phone that he had to take in the next room. I think she was calling. I got a few hang-ups when he was in the garage working on the car. I don't know. I just go over and over it. I think I'm going nuts. Mainly, I can't stop imagining them having sex and what they are doing to each other. I always thought we had a good sex life. Now when we have sex, I freeze up. I feel that I should be sexier now, and show him. I try to be very passionate, but I am not reacting to him. It's a performance. And then I lose it, because I can't get the picture of them together out of my mind."

Just as you review your time together and try to remember his words and what they mean, she does something similar. You both are trying to make sense of a situation, trying to understand what your future will be.

Trust

She has been betrayed, and she will be suspicious of his comings and goings. Her first internal reaction is one of disbelief. She is stunned and shaken. Her second reaction is to want an accounting of how he spends his time and if you are any part of it. This is not unreasonable. On a scale of one to ten on trust, she places him now at zero. I have known women who have asked their husbands to take a polygraph (lie detector) test to check on whether the affair is continuing. If their marriage is to be rebuilt, she must be assured that she can trust him. How can trust ever be re-established? Trust is not rebuilt easily or quickly. There are two elements necessary to begin that process. He must express feelings of remorse, and he must be willing to cooperate to repair the marriage.

If his relationship with you is a fling, and he does not want his marriage to end, he will meet these two requirements. Most men begin very cooperatively in the process of building trust, but at some point down the line they may object. They begin to feel discouraged, thinking it will never end.

> *Steve:* "I will always be made to feel terrible over this. When will she ever stop checking up on me?"

However, it is necessary for her recovery. The husband now must become part of the healing process.

If he does not stop seeing you, he may be ambivalent about his marriage or about your relationship, he may be experiencing your relationship as a romantic love affair, or he may be a poor-risk partner who is not truthful with either you or his wife.

Apologizing

He will apologize repeatedly to her, but it will not be accepted early in this process. He will need to apologize many times and it must cover some important ground to be accepted. In my opinion, he owes you an apology as well, and if the affair is ending he must bring closure to it with finality, honesty, and respect.

It will take them about two years to resolve any problems they have, to put his affair to rest, and for them to rebuild and strengthen their marriage.

If this should be the case, you also will have to go through a process to heal. You will feel pain at the loss of your lover and the dreams that were so much a part of your time with him. You can heal and become stronger. In the last part of this book, we will discuss how that is done.

Chapter Four

About Him

*Y*ou have found him. He is the man you want to marry and spend the rest of your life with. But he has taken vows to honor and be faithful to another woman—his wife. Despite the glow of love and desire for happiness you might be experiencing from the affair, you must take time out to understand him and make sense of his behavior toward you. There is much you need to know about him to arrive at the answer to the question, "Will he really leave her to marry me?"

There are three important questions about him for you to explore: How strong is his connection to you? What is the truth about his marriage? and Why hasn't he left his wife to marry you?

How Strong Is His Connection to You?

Gifts, tender kisses, and dinners out won't give you that information. You must understand what this affair means to him. In part you determine this by assessing what kind of an affair it is for him. Let's revisit the types of affairs to see if you can determine how he is experiencing the affair.

The Serial Affair

If it is a serial affair, there is not a strong connection. You are one of many, and you can be sure there will be many after you.

If you find this lover, or any other, has been treating you poorly and without respect, then you need to determine if you have developed a pattern of becoming involved with men who will not be able to join you in a happy and healthy relationship. The first warning sign is that, although he is married, he is having an affair with you. If you are involved with him, you should know the answers to any of the following:

Has he had affairs before meeting you?
Does he flirt with other women?
Is he currently seeing other women as well as seeing you?

If so, you are putting yourself in a position to be treated badly. Not all women having affairs with married men have an idyllic hideaway retreat, a cocoon protecting them from the outside world. There are women who find their relationship to be verbally, physically, or emotionally abusive—or any combination of the three. An abusive man may be hard to spot because he can also be very charming and he can be a respected member of the community. He can be famous and receive prizes for his work, but he can still be self-centered, angry, and disrespectful. If you have been involved with such a person in the past, you must check yourself carefully to see if you are once again so involved. Such a relationship can only end in emotional and/or physical pain for you.

Spotting the Poor-Risk Partner

The poor-risk partner is not a good candidate for a husband or a lover. More women than I can count have told me that there were signs that they ignored and only later realized that they were significant.

Susan: "It was like looking through a keyhole of a door. I saw a beautiful room, but didn't pay attention to the details. I was aware that there would be consequences if I didn't do what he wanted. I wouldn't see or hear from him for a while. It would make me crazy. He wouldn't return my phone calls and then when he called, he was so charming and I was so grateful to see him that we just continued from there."

What Susan describes is an emotionally abusive situation in which she felt controlled. There are similarities to a physically abusive situation in which tension builds until he strikes her and then shows remorse. After the remorse, there is a honeymoon period until tension builds again and the cycle is repeated. Not all relationships with poor-risk partners are physically abusive, but they are usually emotionally abusive. Leading a woman on is a form of abuse. It gives him power and control over you. In fact, he may be so charming that you discount other situations that may indicate this is not a good relationship for you. The following questions may help you spot the poor-risk partner:

1. **Anger.** Does he express his anger in a nonaggressive way and review the situation to understand it, or does he go into a rage, want revenge, throw things, or hurt you?
2. **Stability.** Does he seem to have an even temperament, or is he unstable—angry one day and loving the next?
3. **Walking on eggshells.** Are you comfortable with him, or are you anxious because you do not know what to expect?
4. **Communication.** Does he listen to your view, try to understand, and then come to a compromise, or does he express himself without regard to your wishes and then act on his own decisions?
5. **Empathy.** When something happens to you, or to both of you, that upsets him, does he consider how it affects you as well, or does he focus on his own reaction only?
6. **Women.** Is he respectful of women, or is he demeaning in his words and his behavior?
7. **Support.** Does he listen, try to help, and care as you cope with the situation, or does he ignore or minimize your emotional needs?
8. **Future.** When you want to discuss your future, does he listen, or avoid the discussion, get angry, or tell you to wait?
9. **Responsibility.** Does he accept responsibility for mistakes, or does he try to shift the blame to someone else?
10. **Generosity.** Does he pay or share the expenses involved in your relationship, or are you the one paying for everything?
11. **History.** Is this the first time he has cheated on his wife or on any premarital relationships, or does he have a history of infidelity in all his past relationships?
12. **Current fidelity.** Do you believe he is faithful to you, or has he cheated on you in the past or is he cheating on you now?
13. **Honesty.** Do you believe the only lying he does is to his wife about this affair, or do you believe he also lies about other things to you?

14. **Getting his way.** Does he go along with decisions that are discussed, or must decisions go his way or he sulks?
15. **Abuse.** If he is in a bad or angry mood does he find a way to cope, or does he scream at you or push you around?
16. **Law.** Has he been an upstanding citizen, or has he had trouble with the law, and spent time in jail?
17. **Children.** Does he treat children with respect, or does he demean them in words or actions (like not paying child support for his children from a previous marriage) or words?
18. **Sex.** Do you trust him not to pass on a sexually transmitted disease or do you worry silently that he could be having unsafe sex with someone else?

If you have been able to say "yes" to the first part of each sentence, then your lover is probably *not* a poor-risk partner. The second part of each statement indicates that he is a man with problems and there is a good chance he is a poor-risk partner. You may not see these traits when your contact with him is limited. However, they will be more obvious, annoying, and possibly dangerous if he leaves his wife and you spend more time with him. It is important that you sort this through now!

The Fling

If your affair is a fling, then he is most likely very passionate and you both respond with increased self-esteem from being with each other. This can be confusing to you to think it is only a fling, because it is obvious that he loves being with you and finds you very special. It may not, however, be a romantic love affair. *Loving to be with you and loving you are not necessarily the same.*

John loved being with Darlene. He talked about her with the utmost respect and admiration:

"I can't begin to tell you how much I love being with her and what I feel like when I am with her. But, I can't leave Isabelle and marry Darlene. I can't bring myself to tell that to Darlene—then I would lose her. Life just gets too involved. Isabelle and I should not have married, but we did and we still are, and that's what I have to deal with. As difficult as things are, I know her reaction would be horrendous. There is also the finances to think about. We bought a gem of a home out in Rockville and a really expensive neighborhood grew up next to ours, making our house escalate in value. We are working our way up a corporate ladder. Together our salaries give us a nice lifestyle. I'm a realist. Separation means this would change, and I guess I am too comfortable with what I have."

So even though John says he loves Darlene, he can't transform his affair into true love with commitment, and he isn't honest with Darlene about this. He is not even ambivalent. He is clear on what he wants, but he is not sharing that with Darlene. It isn't fair that he will not tell Darlene that he won't leave his wife. Darlene can see he loves being with her and assumes that it is only a matter of time until he leaves Isabelle.

The most difficult fact for you to face is that for him, the affair may be a fling. It is important for you to distinguish a fling from a romantic love affair. The biggest pitfall for you is to mistake the two.

It is important to gauge how truthful your lover is if he promised to marry you, when your relationship still does not seem to be moving in that direction. He probably considers the affair a fling if any of the following apply:

1. He hid or tried to hide his marital state from you.
2. He does not talk or is reluctant to talk about a future for the two of you.
3. If he talks about the future, it sounds like promises, not like plans.
4. When you want extra time together, he finds it difficult to meet your requests.
5. He avoids discussion of marriage.
6. He has a very strong emotional attachment to his family.
7. When you need him in a crisis, you feel he is emotionally, as well as physically, unavailable.
8. You know that he lies to you.
9. You sense that your desire to be with him is greater than his to be with you, even allowing for the difficulties in getting together.
10. You often feel it is the sex rather than being together that is most important to him.

11. There are times you don't hear from him for weeks.
12. You have no way to reach him.
13. The previous conditions that describe your lover still exist after a year or more of being together.

A year is an arbitrary time, picked only to indicate that the affair may be static. As you know, a fling can move up the continuum to become a romantic love affair. If you want an indication that he is moving toward leaving his wife yet you see no changes, then it may very well be a fling. A man in a romantic love affair is torn about his feelings for you and what action he should take, and he discusses this with you.

The Romantic Love Affair

If he experiences this affair as a romantic love affair, then like the lover in the fling, he is passionate in his feeling for you and shows this by wanting to be with you, to touch you, to kiss you, and he thinks of you when he is not with you. But more than that, he cares about your well-being, your future, your growth and development. He wants you to be the most that you can be.

He is intoxicated with you. It does not necessarily mean he is a great lover, but you are for him a great love. He shows emotional intimacy. You have no anxiety about sharing your weaknesses, because you know he will respond with acceptance and concern, and you will still respect each other.

Some Common Mistakes

Even though a fling can develop into a romantic love affair, it is no assurance that he will leave his wife. For many men, the decision to leave a marriage is a struggle and it is shared with their lover, but for others it is not.

Using Control

Rick: "I love Carrie more than I can explain. Maybe I should break it off. I can't decide what to do, but I am thinking about a trial separation. It's a big move to leave a wife and three kids. I've discussed this with Carrie many times. I owe her an answer, but I need to go about this in a responsible way. I want to have the respect of my children. It will hurt Jean. It's not easy."

Rick wants to try a trial separation to test his feelings about leaving his marriage. That is a step toward commitment to Carrie, but one that can be plagued with problems when not done carefully with an understanding of the guidelines and boundaries. By not telling his wife that he is having an affair, he is not being honest with her. He is leaving her out of the equation. He plans to come to a conclusion and tell her only if he decides to leave the marriage. He is trying to control more than he can, or should.

In some ways it is possible to think of a trial separation as a scientific experiment, in that the variables must be controlled. This means that at the end you will know what accounted for your conclusion. Trial separations are difficult because people are not like chemicals in an experiment and there are variables beyond your control, including people's rights. If Rick wants to have some insight, when the trial separation from his wife ends, he needs to stop the affair, tell his wife why he is doing this, maintain his contact with his family, and after an agreed-upon period, evaluate his feelings. His wife will surely have a strong reaction to the news.

If Rick starts his trial separation, his wife will want to know why. No one asks for a trial separation out of the blue. She will be concerned and try to understand his reasons. She will most likely ask for marital counseling. He must be prepared to go for counseling to help her through this crisis. If they are having problems that have not been resolved or she senses he has been remote, his wife may suspect and ask about another woman. A therapist will help set the parameters and expectations about the separation, but must be informed about the affair to be able to help him set any guidelines. Without that knowledge, neither the therapist nor the wife will understand the lack of progress.

The best-case scenario for Rick is to first seek individual counseling to understand why he cannot give up either his affair or his marriage and to learn more about himself. Then he and his wife should work with a therapist to sort through their problems. Although it may be hard for you to understand, this will make Rick feel he has done everything to work on his marital problems if he decides with his wife to end his marriage. If he marries Carrie, he will better understand himself, feel less guilt, and if he has made a mistake in his marriage, he will now have enough knowledge that he will not repeat it.

More Dishonesty

Kurt couldn't give up Marla, and he couldn't give up his marriage:

"Marla and I met at work and we became lovers just from being together and finding out we liked each other and enjoyed the same things. We have been sexually intimate for a year. I am happier with her than with my wife, but I feel I can't leave my marriage. I told Marla and she was heartbroken. So we have gone back to being friends. We meet for lunch on Friday, but there are no stolen weekends or lunch hours. There's no sex, only a peck on the cheek. I look forward to our Friday lunches."

Kurt has decided to stop the affair in a way, but not in a fair way either to his wife or to his lover. He and Marla started their relationship at work with an emotional affair. When sexuality enters an emotional affair, the relationship automatically becomes a romantic love affair because emotional intimacy has already developed. Now that Kurt has decided that he doesn't want to give up his marriage, he finds he can't give up Marla either. So Kurt has devised a way of keeping in contact with Marla that makes him feel he is not having an affair. Actually, they have come full circle and are back to having an *emotional affair*.

Remember, the three components of an emotional affair are sexual chemistry, emotional intimacy, and secrecy. When we view it in terms of Dr. Sternberg's model of true love, we can see how they relate. The sexual chemistry is analogous to passion, and emotional intimacy is present in both models. The significant difference is in the third side of the triangle—commitment. Commitment cannot exist in the presence of secrecy. With Kurt and Marla, passion will no longer be expressed physically, but it will be there in the form of sexual chemistry. Emotional intimacy is present. When a true commitment is made, secrecy changes.

The previous statements of Kurt and Rick show the struggle, and their attempt at a solution. Neither solution is fair to the wife or to the lover. So where does this leave them—and more importantly, where will it lead them? With the first couple, Carrie may eventually be in a power struggle with Rick because he wants to control the affair and the marriage by doing things his way and being dishonest. The second couple, Kurt and Marla, may continue this way for a while and then resume their affair. If the indecision continues, their affair could go on for years and become a *long-term affair*.

The Long-Term Affair

When a couple is having a long-term affair, they have decided to continue as they are, for any number of reasons. One reason is indecision on the part of the husband. There are affairs that never reach a transition or an endpoint.

It is not that easy to maintain a long-term affair for most people because of the realities of life. Long-term affairs present special problems that will be dealt with in Chapter 8, "Continuing with the Affair."

You want him to leave his wife and he has not committed to that. If you feel you both are experiencing your relationship as a romantic love affair or a long-term one and he has not been able to leave her for you, something is holding him back. What is it?

Why Hasn't He Left His Wife to Marry You?

You cannot understand why you two have the same conversation over and over again. To you, he clearly wants this, yet there is always an obstacle, a date, or a reason why it can't be. He seems to want it both ways and you cannot understand this feeling, which we know as ambivalence.

Ambivalence

Ambivalence is a major source of frustration for the woman who wants her lover to leave his marriage and marry her. His ambivalence means that he is feeling conflicted about whether he should stay or go. He says or indicates he will be ending his marriage, but he doesn't. You may assume it is due to consideration of his family. Maybe he says he is waiting for some future event to occur, after which he will be free to leave his wife. When all such dates and events pass and there is no movement for him to leave his marriage, or there is an avoidance of discussion about your future as a married couple, it may be a sign of his ambivalence.

He may fear the opinion of other significant people in his life, like family members, friends, community members, or professional colleagues. Sometimes the future event just buys him time, for he thinks by then he will be able to leave his wife.

For other men it is an excuse to buy time for the affair to continue. He is not planning to leave his wife, or perhaps he *is* planning to leave his wife, *but it may not be for you!*

Attachment to His Family

His ambivalence can be due to many things that you are not aware of. Sometimes the reason for his ambivalence may be that he loves his wife, but has been unable to resolve their problems or his own. His attachment to his marriage is stronger than he realizes. He may also be feeling guilty about the affair and talking about leaving his family.

He has had years with his wife, memories both good and bad that bind them together. If he has children, this is a major source of attachment that for many men is extremely difficult to weaken or sever in any way. Even if his marriage has been difficult, and he feels he would be happier not married, this attachment plays a role in his inability to leave.

The idea of a secret love nest for just the two of you where you can hide from others may give him a feeling of excitement that is just too much for him to give up. He doesn't get that with his wife because of the realities of day-to-day family life. But in the long run, his attachment to his wife and family is too strong to give up.

It's Good to Be the King!

He may be very reluctant to give up this affair and the private world that the two of you have built. It is an exciting time for him, one that may be very different from his home life. With you he feels special, and his self-esteem has taken an immense upward swing. He may have no intention of marrying you, but telling you that will increase the chance that you will leave. So he may not want to tell you the truth.

If this is happening to you, you may be confused or angry. When he is with you, he seems very loving and caring and you believe your private haven is something that he would want to be permanent. But for him, it is perfect—a secret kingdom. It's good to be the king!

Gender Differences: Power and Control

As much as women would like to believe there are no gender differences, anyone who has experience with couples who are coping with infidelity will tell you that men feel that they can separate their feelings about their marriage from their feelings about their affair. That is why many say their affair means nothing to them and that it was just sex. As we have seen, most women equate sex with love, so an affair has more meaning to them. That is why, when the wife has an affair, it is a greater threat to the marriage. It is not just about sex, but about intimacy and strong feelings as well.

Harriett, a wife who discovered the affair, told me, "I can't believe she means nothing to him. Before I would have sex with another man, I would have to have very special feelings for him." The number of younger women responding like Harriett is decreasing as a result of cultural changes, but many women still equate sex with love.

Annette Lawson, in her book *Adultery*, writes that men believe that they can have a parallel marriage and an affair, and that one will not affect the other. This represents control.

Related to this is power. In *Man Enough*, Dr. Frank Pittman writes, "It [infidelity] is a power play, an effort to get something or know something your partner doesn't know."

Leading You On

One of the problems about ambivalence is the difficulty in knowing when it is indecision or an excuse to keep the status quo of your relationship.

Can you tell if his behavior and what he says really mean that he is torn between you and his wife? If he has made a private decision to leave his wife, he may not be sure you are the one for him. Then again he could be leading you on. From his standpoint, he sees that you are enjoying the affair as much as he is and he may want it to continue just as it is. It is only when you pressure him about your future that he becomes reactive.

> *Fannie:* "Our relationship was going downhill. I wanted more from him. I was tired of waiting. He talked about our future together, but never in a definite way. I am racing against a biologic clock that keeps ticking away. I finally spoke out and told him that I wanted to have children and that would be hard if we waited any longer. I was already thirty-eight and not getting any younger. He was forty-five with two kids, so I don't know if it was all that important to him. We had a row over it and then I finally saw the light when he said that I should 'take my thirty-eight-year-old uterus and find some other guy.' I don't know how I so misjudged him."

Fannie was hoping against hope, ignoring the signals, and being treated very poorly by her lover. It is easy to hang on to half-promises and to imagine a future for yourself with someone when your relationship with him is so devoid of reality. Just as he is tricked by the razzle-dazzle of an affair, so are you. It is hard to see reality when neither of you has to deal with the world outside of the narrow confines you have made for yourselves.

Retaliation

Retaliation occurs sometimes as a reaction against a hurt or perceived hurt. It may be that his wife has had an affair, and his retaliation by having an affair evens things out. But he may retaliate because of her harsh words, a feeling of powerlessness in his marriage, or a general atmosphere of hostility at home. It may be that he cannot, or for other reasons will not, give up his marriage. Your affair is a safety valve. It makes his marriage more tolerable. As much as he enjoys this affair, he may have no intention of giving up his marriage, even though the affair is truly a romantic love affair. He is unwilling to make the commitment, the component that would make it true love. Promises and innuendoes about your future together must have some muscle behind them.

How Realistic Is His Promise to Marry You?

This is one of the most important and difficult questions you must ask yourself. If you want him to leave his wife and marry you and you are making plans based on that, or passing up opportunities based on this wish, you must step back and do a reality check. What actions on his part make you believe that he intends to marry you?

> *Amy:* "He talks about the future, the kind of home we will have, the type of lifestyle. He wants to move to a warmer climate."

What Amy's lover is telling her is a vague picture of a life together. Is it "bait and switch" or does he mean it? Time will tell, but asking the right questions might also provide the answers. The right questions would focus on what is left out of his description, and that is the specifics: when, how, where.

If you are afraid to ask these questions, you need to ask yourself why you are afraid to confront your lover about the specifics of your future together.

> *Amy:* "I'm afraid to ask. Maybe I will be pushing him too fast, too far, too soon."

The fear Amy expresses here can mean many things. Maybe Amy herself is ambivalent, or she knows the answer and doesn't want to hear it, or she knows he has been lying to her.

It Runs in the Family

Another indication of future trouble is his role model for monogamy. If he comes from a family where the men are not faithful to their wives, then the possibility exists that he might follow suit. There are families in which infidelity can be seen throughout the generations. As mentioned earlier, the family of President John F. Kennedy is one example. His father, Joseph Kennedy, had a long-term relationship with actress Gloria Swanson, as well as other affairs. The Kennedy daughters married men who had affairs, and some of them came from families in which the men had affairs. The women's role was to tolerate it.

Indications He Is Not Serious

When you see that he continues to make plans with his family for future activities, you can suspect that there may not be any future that will include you.

> *Marci:* "He and Linda took two European vacations each year for the three years I was involved with him. They redecorated their home. I made excuses for him. He was an important man in his firm and he had to entertain. I attributed my hurt feelings to envy, but it was more. How could I question him, I asked myself? I was married too, and I also did family things. I finally had the talk with him that I was too afraid to have. He wasn't going to marry me. He got involved with me because I was safe, since I had a husband and child. He wanted to continue as we were."

The Deadline Passes

When you put your plans and desires aside because you are waiting for something to happen that never does, or the event passes and you are no closer to a change in your arrangement with him, then you are getting a signal.

> *Denise:* "I waited for his job promotion, then his son's bar mitzvah, then his wife's recovery from back surgery before I got suspicious. The hard thing about this is that he seemed sincere and caring. I always thought our time would come."

Being afraid to question is understandable, but being afraid to find out his intentions will only delay your knowledge of what he has in mind and prolong a relationship that will lead you back to where you started.

Cathy: "I am afraid to question him because I may scare him off. What if he tells me something I don't want to hear?"

If you feel like Cathy, then ask yourself how you would feel if this affair were to become a long-term one and then he ended it due to some unforeseen future event. If that feels better to you than frightening him off, then your next question to yourself should be, "What kind of a man is this who can't have a discussion about our future when we are having a sexual relationship?"

He Continues to Find Another Deadline

A variation on the theme is that one event is replaced with another and so your waiting time increases. You never feel like you're on safe ground.

Bobbie: "How I wish I listened to my doubts when he told me that the summer condo he bought for his family in Bethany was just a short-term investment. He would sell it in a few years when the kids were ready for college and the money would be for us. So when he sold it, the money he made went for his children's education. Where was my head on this? I had enough divorced girlfriends to know what goes on. That money should have been for our future together. I wanted to believe him. It sounded so great."

He Avoids That Serious Talk

When you sense that he changes the subject, puts off the talk, or just won't have that talk, you can be sure that he doesn't want to be pinned down. As far as he is concerned, things are going well.

Cynthia: "He promised me we would talk about the future. We were going to dinner and back to my apartment to talk. We went to dinner, but he had to leave for an unexpected late meeting and so we couldn't have the talk. Life with him was like that. Something always came up. I didn't press it because I was afraid of his answer. We both somehow swept it under the carpet."

He Makes Deals

Making deals that show you are not a priority indicates that he is not making himself free for you.

Ilene: "I wanted to spend Christmas with him in some way. Thanksgiving came and went and I was alone and just imagining the great dinner he and his family were having. I asked for part of his Christmas. I would be willing to take whatever he had to offer. I suggested a brunch, a lunch, a coffee hour. I was also dreading New Year's Eve. I knew it would be horrible. He told me it was very risky because Liz was very suspicious and always checking on him, now that she knows about us. He clinched it when he told me that if he were not there on New Year's Eve, her crazy brother would get back at me. When I asked how, he said he didn't know, but he thought he used drugs and was unstable."

If you see your life like chapters, each defined by one reason, excuse, or delay, then at some point you will question his seriousness concerning your future together.

If you have already figured out he is a poor-risk partner, a philanderer, or someone having a fling, then you know there will be no signs that he is serious about leaving his wife and marrying you. He may tell you he will, but the probability of his doing so and the prospects of a successful marriage are not high. On the other hand, there may be indications that he does truly care as much about your future as you do.

Indications That He Is Serious

Just as there are signs that he is not going to leave his wife, there are signs that he is seriously considering it or that he is struggling with a decision. This usually happens, as we have discussed, when he is experiencing your relationship as a romantic love affair.

Open Discussions with You

Rather than avoiding a discussion, he is honest in telling you that it is a major decision to leave his wife and family and he wants to be certain he is doing the right thing for the right reasons. Therefore, he tells you that he is going to be doing some serious thinking about what to do. He may tell you that he loves you, but that doesn't mean the right course of action is to leave his family and marry you without carefully thinking about it. This may be hard for you to hear. You want him to sweep you into his arms and tell you he is leaving her to marry you, but you need to keep in mind that he is taking a big step and needs to know you support him in his quest for understanding. You need to make it safe for him to speak to you. Good listening skills and careful introspection at this point will be better for you in the long run.

> *Jack:* I want to talk to you about something important.
> *Loretta:* What? This sounds serious.
> *Jack:* I am very confused about what to do about Jenny and the kids. Sometimes I want to leave and other times I feel like a heel. I know I love you. So I found a therapist and I am going to talk to him so I know I am doing the right thing.
> *Loretta:* Are you going to go with Jenny?
> *Jack:* No. We've done that a few times. I need to go by myself.
> *Loretta:* Can I go with you?
> *Jack:* No.
> *Loretta:* You're leaving me, aren't you?
> *Jack:* No. I am trying to decide if I should leave my marriage.
> *Loretta:* And marry me?
> *Jack:* Maybe. First, I need to make a decision about leaving.
> *Loretta:* And what do I do? Wait around?

Jack: I would like you to give me some time. Do you think that's fair?

Loretta: What are we talking about? A year?

Jack: Let's try for three months.

Loretta: This is hard, Jack. I don't know if I can do it.

Jack: Give me three months and maybe I'll know something. At least, we will talk about it then and see where we are. I would like to have your support on this because you mean so much to me.

Loretta: But not enough to marry?

Jack: Enough to marry, but there are others I need to consider.

Loretta: Okay. Only because I love you.

This is an example of how a conversation can go. It causes Loretta's anxiety to rise. She thinks this is the beginning of the end, but that is jumping to conclusions. She is asked to wait three months and then they will evaluate their relationship. Loretta is being supportive despite her fears.

He Starts Counseling

One of the most hopeful signs for all involved is if he would seek psychological counseling for himself. There are many reasons for this:

1. He recognizes that he has had personal problems that have repeatedly kept him from having stable relationships, with friends, family, and colleagues at work. It would be beneficial for him, and for you as well, to sort through this so he can gain an understanding of himself, resolve these issues, and learn coping skills. Then if you two marry, he will not be repeating problems he and his wife may have had in their marriage. Second marriages have a higher divorce rate than first ones. This is, in large part, because people repeat their mistakes. They marry for the second time when their relationship is in the passion stage and they mistake that for true love. Think of the many mistakes you avoided by not marrying someone you once had a relationship with when you were in the early, highly charged passion stage. You may have seen that person after the relationship was over and realized that you saved yourself from some misery.

Because an affair is high in passion, you must be sure to keep a clear head and iron out any serious wrinkles before a commitment.

2. If he has problems in his marriage, it is vital for him to really know what they are about. His seeing a therapist may feel like a risk to you because it may be that he can work those problems out. If he finds he cannot, then he can leave his wife, knowing why he did so with the knowledge that he has done everything he could to avoid a divorce in his family. Most of all, he understands what the problems are. This means being truthful with his wife about his affair. It also means that the counseling will include helping her to heal from his betrayal.

3. If he recognizes his ambivalence and wants to understand it, then he is making positive efforts to know why he is not leaving. He may find out and then be able to make the commitment to leave, or he may discover he cannot make the commitment. In the long run, it will be to your advantage that he knows those things about himself. A question for you is: How much time do you want to give to someone who cannot bring himself to commit?

Judy: "I was frightened when he went for counseling. I didn't see the point. He knew he hated her nagging. The therapist taught them communication skills and made other changes, but it soon became apparent there were differences in their outlooks and what they wanted from life that he couldn't provide and she was unwilling to compromise on. So it was better to have gone for counseling. The ending was more or less mutual. She hated him for having the affair with me, but they agreed to separate."

Not all counseling ends in this way. Sometimes the married couple reconciles and works out their differences. However, if he does not try to salvage his marriage, he may have suppressed feelings of guilt that may later surface as hostility toward you. The advantage of therapy is that a difficult transition like divorce can be done in a more responsible way. This is very important, since it can impact negatively on the children, and for generations to come. The advantage to this for you is that you will marry a man who knows he has done everything he could to save his marriage. You will marry a man who has worked to gain an understanding of himself and who has learned coping skills that will help in the future.

If he recognizes that his own personal problems have brought him to the point of being unfaithful to his wife, he should understand what these problems are all about before embarking on a new marriage. "Those who forget the lessons of history are condemned to repeat them," said philosopher George Santayana. If his history is one filled with problems, the chance of a successful marriage to you can only improve from such introspection.

Separation

The next step for him is to move into an apartment by himself, *not* to move in with you. He needs some "space" because he is going through a major life transition and will need a temporary place until his emotions stabilize. In this process, he must leave his family in a responsible way by maintaining regular and consistent contact with his children. And if later he and his wife should divorce, he must make timely and complete payment of his child support and other financial obligations, share custody of his children, and be emotionally available to them. He must also help in the decision-making that affects them. Instead of resentment, this should win him your respect for his maturity.

If he abandons his family or shows little interest in them, your expectations of your life with him should be reduced. You would be wise to re-evaluate your involvement with him. If he goes for counseling to sort things out, as frightening as it might seem to you, you are going to marry a man who has tried to make a responsible transition with regard to his wife and children, and you can respect him for that.

Premarital Counseling

Having an affair is like suspending reality. If at this point you decide to marry, I strongly advise premarital counseling. All the irritants, little daily problems, personal habits will now come into focus. It will require work to adjust to reality rather than clandestine romantic interludes. Annoyances can become magnified when people are living so closely together.

Additionally, you will become part of his larger family. You will be a stepmother if he has children and you will have other roles as well, such as daughter-in-law, sister-in-law, and aunt. You will now be going through a major life transition, and that is stressful. Remember the working definition of a transition that we are using. It is "a new set of assumptions about your world, yourself, and your future." As you can see, this will apply to you.

> *Shirley:* "We knew each other for years before we became romantically involved. He is *my* dream guy; he and his wife did not get along from the start. We didn't move right in together after his divorce. It was months later. Well, he has these habits I never knew about and it is driving me crazy, like cutting his fingernails and leaving the cuttings all over. Or not answering me when I tell him I am going out. We can't agree on a vacation spot. He wants to camp. Yeah, right! I want room service. I want to go to a little arty getaway. When I think about it, they are not such big deals, but somehow when you live with someone so closely they are magnified. I am turning into the kind of person I don't want to be. I wonder if this has been a mistake and I wonder if he thinks that too. Then we have a wonderful romantic evening and I think I'm nuts."

These are typical problems of adjustment that newlyweds have. Premarital counseling will make each person aware of the other's priorities as well as what they feel they can or cannot compromise on. The couple will learn communication skills and help them put procedures into place that will ease this transition.

I have found that the majority of couples I have worked with really enjoy premarital counseling and benefit from it. Now they are ready for marriage, but there will be other issues that will arise and that we will explore in Chapter 9, "You and He Marry."

There are many concerns about life together that almost every couple has before they marry. You are entering this relationship with a major concern stemming from your secret relationship: *Can I trust him not to cheat and not to lie?* Dishonesty goes hand in hand with infidelity. Infidelity, by definition, is dishonesty. If he cheats, he may also lie. The issue of honesty must be looked at separately. You need to look back at your relationship and see if it was dishonest in other ways.

Will He Cheat on You?

Since the best predictor of future behavior is past behavior, you have every reason to have doubts about his ability to be faithful to you. If this is his first extramarital affair and if he has a history of being honest with the women with whom he has been involved, and not cheated in those relationships, then your chance of his being faithful improves. If as a single man he treated a woman dishonestly, was not faithful to her when he was in a serious relationship, and if he has had previous extramarital affairs, the probability increases that he will cheat on you.

His general attitude about infidelity is important to observe. If his friends are unfaithful to their wives and he sees this affair as a lark or macho thing to do, then you know he does not take fidelity seriously.

If his wife allows the affair to go on and looks the other way, it will be expected of you as well. Such behavior in families does not have to continue from generation to generation, however. It can stop. Infidelity is a choice. Individuals have the capacity to accept or reject behavior. Many of the grandchildren of Joseph Kennedy have rejected infidelity—but others have not.

If he has personality traits similar to those listed in the description of the poor-risk partner, then the chances are slim that he will be faithful to you. Repeated affairs cannot be ignored. In *Surviving Infidelity*, Gloria Harris and I wrote:

> "Dick Morris, former presidential adviser, testified before the grand jury that he called the president after reading accounts of the Lewinsky matter. Mr. Clinton confided to Morris, 'You know, ever since the election, I've tried to shut myself down. I tried to shut my body down sexually, I mean. . . . But sometimes, I slipped up with this girl. I just slipped up.'
>
> "This is not the first time that the American public learned of presidential infidelity. In 1998, many public television stations aired *The President's Collection*. The special program on the

Kennedys explored the sexual appetites of President John F. Kennedy. Priscilla McMillan, a staff member for Kennedy when he was a senator, reported her conversation with him: 'Jack, when you are straining every gasket to be elected president, why do you endanger it by going out with women?' He thought about it and replied, 'Because I just can't help it.'"

My experience with women is that they try to be understanding and accepting of others, and because of this they sometimes push aside those nagging doubts and don't really check them out. Cheating on one's spouse is abusive to her and to the family. If you see the following behaviors in your lover, you can consider yourself in the Infidelity Danger Zone:

Infidelity Danger Zone
1. When he was single, he cheated while having a serious relationship.
2. He has had previous affairs as a married man.
3. He has been divorced twice and is now cheating on his third wife.
4. He flirts with other woman.
5. His friends have had affairs.
6. His father, brothers, or uncles have had affairs.
7. His attitude about affairs is lighthearted.
8. He takes you for granted.
9. You often catch him lying to you.

If your answer is "yes" to these questions, you and your lover could be in the Infidelity Danger Zone. This indicates that a serious discussion is needed. As you read further in this book, you will learn the skills to have such a discussion and will learn more about this subject so that you can have an informed discussion with him. In Chapter 10, there is more information about making an Infidelity Contract with each other. For now, you need to deepen your understanding of this situation.

Each person in the marital triangle of an affair—you, your lover, and his wife—is in a transition. When the affair is revealed, it changes the equilibrium for all three. Now, each one of you will have a new assumption about yourself, and your future.

Chapter Five

About You

*I*t is wise to think through what is happening and where it will take you. We all have hopes, dreams, and goals for our future, and it is natural to wonder if we are meeting them. In fact, it is prudent to take time at intervals to see if you are on a course that will make your hopes materialize.

In everyone's life, events happen that are beyond our control, but it is possible to take stock of what we are doing and make necessary changes, because we are *thinking* human beings. Even when our emotions are high, it is possible to look at the events in our life to see if they are harming us or moving us toward our goals. President Clinton's legacy was tarnished because he didn't think through his goals. Or, consider how Catherine Howard, who cheated on King Henry VIII, not only lost her position as queen of England, but literally lost her head as well.

So this is the point where we stand back and honestly look at what is happening in your life. I will present questions and ideas for you to think carefully about and answer honestly. If you are able to use as much objectivity as you can muster, then you can get a sense of where your affair is heading. As we reported previously, Annette Lawson's studies indicate that only about 10 percent of individuals having an affair will leave their spouse to marry their lover. Others put it as low as 1 percent. So we know the probability of his leaving his wife for you is very low. Is the desire to be with him "hoping against hope"?

To know where you stand, you will need to be aware of his behavior, look for patterns, and try to be objective in understanding what is really happening. Because understanding yourself is vital to making decisions, we will start with your own beliefs. Then we will review your relationship, using critical thinking to make a thoughtful assessment.

Tricking Yourself

We have ways to trick ourselves when the pain of the truth will be unbearable. Through this process, we create what is called *defense mechanisms*. It is an unconscious process that we use to protect ourselves against this pain. Knowing the truth would cause more anxiety than we believe we can handle. So the truth is falsified in some way, but we are not aware we are doing it. We cannot allow ourselves to know the truth. Women in this marital triangle frequently use the defense mechanisms of denial and rationalization, as well as minimization, which is a cognitive distortion.

Denial. This happens when we deny what the facts show us to be true. It may be too painful to recognize that his wife and children come first, so you just will not allow yourself to see it. Denial makes unacceptable wishes and facts acceptable. You've probably seen others deny a situation that is obvious to everyone else.

> *Jane:* "I never saw the connection between canceling our meetings and getaways as an indication of his interest in his family over me."

> *Libby:* "I know him. He doesn't have sex with his wife."

Minimization. Although this is not a defense mechanism, it is related to denial. It is actually a cognitive distortion that is a way of changing the truth. In this case it makes it easier to accept. We use it somewhat like a defense mechanism, however, but rather than being unconscious, it is a bridge to reality. The individual recognizes what is happening, but minimizes the effect it will have on her. It is a distortion in thinking.

> *Jane:* "Those getaways are not that important."

> *Gerri:* "I know he wants to end it, but I can handle it. It wasn't that important in my life."

Rationalization. This is a way to explain away something that is really very hurtful or that we cannot accept. It is also protective and employed to prevent the anxiety we would feel if we really understood the meaning of this event in our lives.

Libby: "If he has sex with his wife, it is only so she won't suspect an affair."

Liza: "Why should I feel guilty? If he weren't having this affair with me, he would be having it with someone else."

Teresa: "He couldn't spend our anniversary with me because a man in his position has so many commitments and claims on his time. In my heart, I know he was thinking of me that day."

You can imagine the pain if they had said:

Jane: "He cancels the meetings because he would rather be with his family than with me."

Gerri: "This is a major blow. My heart is broken."

Libby: "He has sex with both of us."

Liza: "This affair is hurting innocent people."

Teresa: "He wouldn't spend our anniversary with me because it is not important to him."

Checking Your Belief System

Many of the beliefs that the lover typically has about the affair are either mistaken assumptions, denials, minimization, or rationalizations. Mostly they tend to deceive her about the facts and the enormity of the repercussions for all involved. Following are a few of the beliefs that women may hold. Check your beliefs against these and then read the facts.

Beliefs

1. An affair with a married man is understandable if you know that he is in an unhappy marriage.
2. An affair with a married man will give him some pleasure and so make his marriage more tolerable.
3. An affair with a married man who is unhappy is permissible because if I weren't the one having the affair with him someone else would be.
4. An affair with a married man doesn't hurt anyone if it is done discreetly.
5. An affair with a married man is not looked down upon in today's world.
6. When push comes to shove, he will choose the person who gives him the most pleasure and fewest problems.
7. I can keep him interested because I am (a) younger, (b) prettier, (c) sexier, (d) more fun, (e) all of the above.
8. I have a special hold on him that a wife can't possibly have.

These beliefs need to be checked out against the facts to see if they are valid. The truth is essential to your happiness. It is crucial to recognize that *your lover may be a partner with you* in maintaining an unchallenged belief system. In the long run, your recognition of the truth is your defense against continuing in a situation that may eventually cause you pain.

Facts

1. You cannot know for certain if his marriage is unhappy. Just because he tells you this does not make it true. Many people who report their marriage is unhappy are not telling the truth. He might think you would be less inclined to end the affair if you thought that an unhappy marriage might cause him to file for divorce. So it is in his interest to allow you to think he is unhappy. Additionally, many men stay in their "unhappy marriages" for other reasons.
2. "Happiness" is highly subjective. People have different perceptions of happiness. He can be happy to be with you, but that doesn't mean he is unhappy at home. Women have been raised to think a man will bring them happiness. Actually, we can be happy to be with someone, but each of us is responsible for our own happiness. We cannot

assume the task of making someone else happy. From my years of counseling women, I will tell you that at first, women do not want to hear that they are responsible for their own happiness. Eventually they come to know it is true. Most come to realize that it is better to count on yourself, than someone else, for your happiness.

3. Assuming he was really unhappy in his marriage, it may be true that he would have an affair with someone else if you were not there. If a man is unhappy in his marriage, his first responsibility is to find out why this is so. It may not have anything to do with his wife. If you were married to him, and he told you he was not happy, would you think it would help him if he cheated on you, or would it help to seek the cause of his unhappiness? The cause of his unhappiness may have nothing to do with his wife, but much to do with him.

4. An affair always hurts a marriage while it is going on and for some time after, because it robs the couple of time together, intimacy, honesty, and good memories. It hurts them in the aftermath in a very profound way. It is devastating to his wife, children, and relatives. They can become stronger, but they'll still have the memory of the affair. It can hurt you if it ends, because you will have invested much of your heart in him, and your dreams of the future together will have been shattered. One example is the affair President Clinton had with Monica Lewinsky. Monica had dreams of a future with him, and in the end she had heartbreak. We saw photographs of Hillary Clinton and their daughter, Chelsea, devastated at the news. But today they have rebuilt their lives together, while Monica is still searching for hers.

5. The public view of affairs is changing, according to the statistics. But it is still looked down upon. In *The Janus Report on Sexual Behavior*, Drs. Samuel S. Janus and Cynthia L. Janus write that in their survey of 2,759 men and women from 1988 to 1992, 83 percent disagree or strongly disagree with the statement, "Extramarital affairs do not seriously affect marriages." The results showed that of the 2,760 people polled in the same time period, 91 percent agree or strongly agree with another statement: "The family is the most important institution in society."

6. Earlier in this book, we reviewed the reasons why he might not choose his lover over his marriage, even though the pleasure

factor in the affair is high. That probability of leaving increases if he believes he is having a romantic love affair and may not be offset by other considerations of his marriage. I have seen marriages of twenty to forty years, in which he leaves his wife and marries his lover. However, the statistics indicate that most of the time, he does not marry his lover.

7. You may be able to keep him interested because you are young, pretty, sexy, and/or fun, but his wife may have the same attributes, even though he may not share this with you. If you were to lose any of these attributes, would he still be interested? All of them can attract him, but it is not the reason he has an affair. The affair satisfies his emotional needs, such as narcissism, power, and low self-esteem.

8. You do have a special hold on him that his wife can't possibly have, because of the nature of an affair. But she has her own special hold because of their years together and the history that is uniquely their own. I have seen men who respect their wives for what they have been through together. Her power in this regard cannot be minimized. In response to *The Janus Report*'s 1988 to 1992 survey statement, "My spouse/partner is also my best friend," 85 percent of the 770 men answered "yes," and 82 percent of the 802 women answered "yes."

It must have been hard for you to read this section. It was hard for me to write it, because it might cause you pain, which is not my goal. In spite of the small percentage of stories of the lover and the husband marrying, from everything that I have heard in my office, or read by those who have "been there, done that," the message is "Stop! You will be hurt!" As wonderful as the affair may be, the pain of the breakup will seem more unbearable the longer it goes on. Your desire to marry him may be strong, but marrying you may not be part of his thinking.

Boundaries

Think back over your first meeting. Did you know he was married? Many women, married or single, meet a man and find that he is fun or interesting to talk to. The encounter with him may have left you with a nice feeling, a sense of intrigue, and a desire to know him better.

What do you remember from your first meeting with him? Was he wearing a wedding ring? Did he mention his wife and children? A wedding ring sends the message, "I am off-limits." It sets up a boundary that should not be crossed. Did you notice the boundaries? If so, did you observe the message they intended to send? Boundaries are very important in our relationships with people. They convey our beliefs and give us a means of defining ourselves. In a relationship, the boundaries need to be clear. Some men do not want to wear a wedding ring, and this can be a red flag. A wedding ring is a very clear symbolic boundary.

Boundaries are established by behavior and through verbal and nonverbal communication. When we speak in innuendo, or respond flirtatiously to someone else, we send a signal that the boundaries are loose. When someone flirts, touches you more than casually, makes private jokes, or acts as though you and he share something special, he is saying something about his boundaries—that they are weak, blurred, undefined, or open. When he doesn't mention that he has a wife and family and is very charming in his interactions with you, a flag should go up, and you need to pay attention to it.

In the following scenario, Glenda and Luke bump into each other at the buffet table at a regional conference they both are attending:

Glenda: *(Laughing)* Sorry. I'm a hungry klutz.
Luke: I thought a klutz was an old man. *(Winking)* You're the best-looking klutz I've ever seen.

Luke continues to be engaging and invites Glenda to join him at his table. By the end of the evening, Luke is telling her jokes, touching her hand, and making plans for them to spend the next day together.

Glenda: *(Fishing)* What would your wife think of you spending time with me?
Luke: *(Dodging)* You see a wedding band? *(He holds up his ringless hand.)*

Glenda does not pursue this further. She and Luke start an affair, and three months later Glenda finds out about his marital status when he is paged with a family emergency and she can hear the conversation.

Glenda is angry and feels deceived, but she continues the affair without considering the true implications.

Luke was actively looking for an affair—first by not wearing his wedding ring and then by diverting Glenda's "fishing expedition" with a joke. To Luke, Glenda signaled her own disregard for boundaries by not going further with the inquiry.

In another situation, Barbara met Joey at a house party and each knew that the other was married. Their spouses were also at the party. The next day, Joey called Barbara under the pretext of finding out some information about her nontraditional treatment for tennis elbow. They met for lunch to discuss it, and eventually they became lovers. It was not Barbara's first affair. She liked having affairs with married men, because it lessened any chance of complications. Eventually, however, Barbara fell in love with Joey, but he set a boundary by not talking about his wife and not asking about Barbara's husband. This most likely says, "Leave my wife out of this." For Joey, it is an affair—it isn't going anywhere.

We know why Barbara looked for a married man. She was open about it later in their relationship, but we don't know Glenda's reasoning. When she found out Luke was married, why did she stay around? This is a very important point for women who have affairs with married men to recognize and eventually understand. Having an affair with a married man is a choice. It may feel to you that "it just happened," but it didn't. It is a way of tricking yourself by denying the truth. Many women say that, but if boundaries were observed it couldn't just happen. Since the statistics indicate it will not work out, it is important to check out your belief system about how you first became involved. Did he send you messages that he was available, when he wasn't? Were his verbal and nonverbal communications clear? Did you ignore his boundaries?

On the other hand, many women start out to catch their lover. The woman sets up a trap and then he falls for the bait, which is her beauty, sex appeal, carefree attitude, and the message, "I am a lot of fun." He is appealing to her and his attention gives a boost to her self-esteem, just as her attention does for him. He may or may not be movie-star handsome, but he has a certain kind of appeal for her. One source of the attraction may be the very fact that he is married. This possibility is something you need to be aware of, and to explore in depth.

Why Married Men?

Could this be happening to you? You need to look back on your relationships and see if you notice a pattern. Do you have a history of becoming involved with married men, or with men who are unavailable in any other way? If so, have you fallen in love with any of the men? Has the relationship broken up because he would not leave his wife for you? If this has been happening to you, then you need to realize that you are in a cycle that ends with your pain. The cycle is this:

1. You are attracted to him and he returns the attention.
2. You know he is married or you find out later in the relationship that he is.
3. His being married does not deter you for more than a little while, or not at all.
4. You tell yourself that he is not happy in his marriage because he is having an affair with you in which he is very attentive and seems to be very passionate and satisfied.
5. You begin to hope that he will leave his wife.
6. You start to think about him leaving his wife and marrying you.
7. Then you start to talk about it.
8. The relationship begins to show instability. There are arguments.
9. You break up and reunite a number of times.
10. For most, eventually the affair ends.
11. You are heartbroken.

In the next chapter, the dynamics of this relationship will be discussed more fully. For now, the big question to ask is, Why do you repeat this cycle with married men? Married men are unavailable. You keep getting involved with married men even though you know it will probably not work out, you will live a life of secrecy and dishonesty, you will be given the pejorative label of "the other woman," you will hurt another family, you will be putting your goals on hold or delaying them until it may be impossible for them to materialize, and you will be left brokenhearted. Why would you cause yourself this pain?

Loving the Same Man Over and Over Again

Another important assessment you must make is to determine if you are falling for the same man over and over again. Not really the same man, but the same type. Many women fall in love with an older man because some of the traits of the older man are appealing. He may be a man who is in a position of power, whom others look up to, and whom you admire. This can make you feel good about yourself. It is self-affirming that a man who has the admiration of so many considers you attractive and exciting enough to have a love affair with. You feel special.

When he is much older than you, it is a distinct possibility that he reminds you of your father. This may be unconscious. Many women who are repeatedly involved in affairs with older men are searching for a kind and loving father figure because their father was not kind and loving, but remote and distant. They seek out what was missing in their childhood, but they usually end up unconsciously choosing a man who is just like their father, but is unavailable because he is married. That unavailability makes it seem safe. This, in part, explains the ambivalence of some women. Some women believe they want their lover to marry them, but their behavior shows that not to be the case. Either they pick an unavailable man or a man who is too much like their father for comfort, and then may act in ways to sabotage the relationship to avoid the intimacy they fear.

On the other hand, some women may pursue relationships to correct and resolve the past. This type of behavior in such relationships is the repetition compulsion. This is when we repeatedly put ourselves in the same unhappy situation of the past to try to get it right or resolve it. For example, a woman who had a cold, critical mother may pick women friends with the same traits, thus re-creating the relationship she had with her mother. She keeps working at it to try to get it right. Relating this to women who have affairs with older men, they re-create a relationship in which their past needs for nurturing were not met, in an attempt to have them met in the present. Again, the woman finds that it doesn't work because her lover is like her father—busy, emotionally unavailable, and attached to another woman. She has unconsciously set herself up for failure. Alternately, perhaps it is her mother's relationship with her father that she is trying to correct in the present.

Gloria Vanderbilt, in her memoir *It Seemed Important at the Time*, writes of her life of love affairs, many with married men, starting early in her life and continuing during the time of writing her book at the age of eighty-one. "Where should I begin? Not at the beginning—that's no fun. Nor at the end, because my story is far from over."

The beginning was no fun for Gloria Vanderbilt. She was the poor little rich girl who was brought up by others, but longed for her mother. In her memoir, she recognizes that her mother did not have the ability to be the mother a little girl needs, and she understands as well that she spent her life involved in love affairs, as well as many marriages, searching from man to man for the love that she so desperately wanted, needed, and deserved from her mother. She writes, "And although I accept that it was not in her nature to ever be capable of this, the longing is so deep in my nature that I have to constantly resist being drawn to men and situations to once again replay the old scenario, always believing that this time the fairy tale will have a happy ending."

Understanding the past and trying to work on those relationships can heal past wounds. Re-creating that relationship through affairs, trying to make it work this time, will not resolve the underlying issue. It is in your best interest to recognize their influence on your present relationships and to know that change is possible. A look back can help with this relationship and others.

Searching

Some people spend a lifetime involved in one relationship after another because they are searching for a misguided resolution of a past relationship or a distraction from the pain it caused. It is important to recognize and deal with the following issues in a more effective way:

- If you see yourself, like Gloria Vanderbilt, on a course of affairs with married men or older men, and you believe you are searching for the love of a parent . . .
- If you see yourself as a woman who is searching and you have been sexually abused as a child and there was no one to protect you or understand the enormity of what happened . . .

- If you grew up in a home searching for encouragement, acceptance, and responsible care, and your needs were ignored . . .
- If you felt childhood shame because your parents neglected you because of their own problems . . .
- If you were searching for peace from the memory of physical abuse by your siblings or your parents . . .

It is important to bring peace into your life now by ridding yourself of these demons. None of this is a reflection upon you. It is important, affair or no affair, to deal with past injustices. Not all affairs are triggered by such a search—a search for relief from pain—but many are.

Even if you are happy in your affair if the past haunts you, as it easily could, find someone to help you understand why this happened and to realize that as a child, you were entitled to more.

Many of the exercises and concepts you will read in this book can be a beginning to relief from the search.

Looking at Behavior

Let's look at some of your feelings and behavior regarding your relationship with your lover and try to understand them as they pertain to your future. Your life has probably changed in many ways since your relationship with him began. At times, you may find yourself feeling as though you are on a seesaw. One minute you're up, feeling exhilarated and on top of the world. The next, you feel low and without the strength to get back that wonderful feeling. I believe this is because you are in a situation in which life with him seems as though it is one paradox after another. There is a push and pull that can feel confusing and keep you off balance.

The Paradoxes
The world of paradoxes that you find yourself in may be confusing to you because the positive aspects are very reinforcing and bring you happiness. Breaking through this deception is difficult, but it must be done so that you understand your situation. Yet the negative aspects

contradict this feeling. So while you are in the throes of romance and excitement, you tend to minimize or discount the negative. But they must be examined with your clear thinking.

Following are some of the paradoxical feelings that keep you in this state of disequilibrium.

Special, but stigmatized

You and he are creating a romantic life together, doing things that build memories. You have anniversaries that commemorate your first meeting, souvenirs from trips you took together, his e-mails, photos of enjoyable times together, all the cards, notes, and gifts he has given you that signify this exciting romance. But in your heart, when you allow yourself time for your innermost feelings, you are hurt because you know there is a stigma attached to this romance. The secrecy of your life together says something is wrong and we must hide and live "life in the shadows."

At times you cannot believe that this has happened to you. You feel that you do not fit that negative stereotype of the sexy siren. You feel special to him, but are well aware of the stigma attached to the role you are now playing. There are very few places in his world, if any, where he can acknowledge you or show acceptance of you and the relationship you both share. He becomes extremely important to you in this relationship. You feel he must validate you if you are having concerns about what you mean to him—but he cannot do this publicly. So while you seem special, you are also stigmatized.

Treasured, but used

The feeling of being treasured is tainted because on some level you feel you are being used. If sex is a very important part of your relationship, you may wonder at times if that is the reason he is with you. It adds excitement and intrigue. You are available for sex, either on the agreed-upon days when you always meet or whenever he can manage to see you. You cannot help but wonder, if sex were not always available, would you still be so treasured? Would just being with you be enough?

Free, but a prisoner

Perhaps the most difficult paradox of all is that you feel free from the rat race of trying to find a relationship, but you are not the free person you thought you would be because you are "on call." Your cell phone plays a very important role in your life. You can always be reached. His time is not his own—he has a wife, family, and job that come first. He works you in whenever he can arrange it. There are emergencies that come up in his life that he must attend to. It is different if you are the one with the emergency. He cannot be there for you if you are suffering from a disappointment of some sort or if he must attend his daughter's ballet recital that night. When you need emotional support, he may not be able to provide that even by phone. On the other hand, you must be on standby for when he can arrange to fit you into his schedule. You give up events because they might conflict with the time when he can see you. So while you are free, you are a prisoner.

A haven of secrecy, but a world of isolation

You are now living a life of secrecy in which something very important has happened and you cannot share this with anyone. When you are excited about this relationship or you think you are in love, the most natural reaction is to tell the world just as Gene Kelly does in the classic scene from *Singin' in the Rain.* It is a natural reaction but one that is denied you. Some can confide in a close friend, but a lot depends on who the man is and how you know him.

You are unable to introduce him to your family because you are embarrassed and also because you know that he would be very disturbed if the news got out. It would definitely cause him problems in his marriage, work, or community. This has a number of consequences. A positive one is that it is exciting and feels romantic that only the two of you know about it and share a secret world. And so, as it becomes more special, it becomes even more isolating.

A zone of safety, yet a web of danger

This feels wonderful because you have created a zone of retreat where you believe you are protected by a lover who cherishes you and the time he spends with you. In actuality, it may not be so safe. You may not be aware of any danger because the secrecy and isolation keeps you from getting feedback from friends who might ask about questionable behavior on the part of your lover. Consequently, you miss out on critical feedback that may prevent heartbreak. So while you feel safe, you may also be in danger.

No longer lonely, but friendless

At last you feel that you have a way to defeat loneliness, but the paradox is that your friends drift away because you now have little time for them. You are no longer free to meet them as often as before. He might call and you must be available, because you don't have as much time with him as you would like. On the occasions when you are with friends, you may act guarded rather than relaxed. Friends sense something is wrong. Their inquiries about how you're doing are met with empty reassurances that satisfy no one and increase the distance that has grown between them and you. So a different kind of loneliness takes hold in your life. While you are no longer lonely, you are without friends.

Justified, but guilty

At times you feel justified in having this affair because you believe that his life is not a happy and satisfying one. He has told you of his marital problems and the difficulties he has with his children. You are the only one he can really pour his heart out to. His family ignores his pain. You feel he trusts you. Even if he doesn't talk about his family and any problems, you may make assumptions that there are many, or else he wouldn't be with you. So you feel justified in meeting his unmet needs, yet you also feel some guilt for having this affair. So you wonder how you can feel both justified and guilty.

Self-esteem, but self-doubt

Your self-esteem is on a roller coaster ride in an affair. The most crucial aspect is whether the way you feel about yourself comes from within or is affair-dependent. It is natural to feel wonderful when someone you have a close relationship to is so complimentary, but good self-esteem needs to come from within. You need to feel good about what you do and who you are, and should not need someone else to be the mirror by which you assess yourself. If feeling good comes from competition with his wife, then your self-esteem is at the mercy of this affair. If it comes only from the affair, it does not come from within you, and it can vanish if the affair ends. So this relationship can paradoxically exist with good self-esteem and self-doubt.

Powerful, but powerless

You have a sense of power and accomplishment because you have caught the attention of a man who has a wife and children. It gives you a feeling of superiority over his wife because you feel you must have the charm and appeal you think that she lacks. In fact, at times you feel like you are his wife and believe that you can make him happy, whereas she obviously cannot. Yet, when you talk about your future, he changes the subject or avoids it or tells you to be patient. You sometimes argue about it and then you wonder what kind of power you really have in the relationship.

When you get really angry and tired of being put off, you may give him an ultimatum. It is ignored or answered with other promises for the future, and then you argue and give him another ultimatum. So your ability to attract him in spite of his having a family gives you a sense of power, yet your inability to persuade him to end his marriage gives you a sense of powerlessness. You feel both powerless and powerful.

What Are You Sacrificing?

You have many feelings about your relationship. Some may be those "nagging doubts," feelings that bother you, but instead of exploring them, you suppress them. However, it is important for you to review your concerns about the affair in light of the facts and to be honest as well as objective.

Are you making personal sacrifices to maintain your affair? In your critical thinking about whether or not this is in your best interest, it is best to look at these sacrifices now, because later, it may be too late. Some of your desires are put on hold with the hope that they will come to fruition, but they may be irretrievable.

Career

There are women who make career choices that are not in their best interest, because of their desire to maintain an affair. Many careers depend on relocation, and some women sacrifice their careers by not making the move. Then they find years later, the affair has ended and the career has stumbled, and regardless of how they try they cannot compensate for the loss. Some women who do move attempt to keep both career and affair. Depending on the individuals, some affairs can continue and even thrive with geographical separation. Other affairs cannot overcome the distance. If it is a major promotion, she will be conflicted. Additionally, she must always hide her feelings, which is not an easy task.

The woman, married or single, who is having an affair with her supervisor or mentor at work loses the daily, frequent contacts with him if she relocates or takes a new position. If she doesn't take the opportunity, her career may not advance as she had hoped, and, additionally, she may cause others to speculate about why she turned down such advancement.

Family

For those women who want to have children, time spent in an affair postpones fulfillment of that desire, sometimes until it is too late. Women are at a greater biologic disadvantage in this regard. For the woman who wants to have a child, knowing the outcome of the affair is crucial. If he doesn't want to marry her, she will have used her precious childbearing years on the wrong guy. She may have time to find the right man, but not time enough to have a child.

Marriage is usually the first priority, but there are women who, if they cannot have him in marriage, will still want to have his children. These women feel they will always be part of his life if they become the mother of his children. But having his child doesn't necessarily mean it will change the outcome especially if he wasn't included in the decision to have a baby. It may very well bring the affair to an abrupt end, leaving the woman to raise the child alone.

Another consideration for many women is whether or not he even wants to have children. As a married man, it is likely that he already has children. He may not want to have children for financial reasons, or because he has already raised one family and doesn't want to do it again. Or he is nearing retirement and considers a new family a setback. On the other hand, there are some men who feel they did it all wrong with the first family, so they welcome the chance to start again and handle it differently. Some older men feel revitalized with a new wife and a young family. They can also show the world how virile they are. It is another boost to their self-esteem.

The only way you will know is by discussing it, and by understanding your life goals and your priorities. If he doesn't want children and you do, you need to evaluate what is most important for you and what you are giving up for the affair. I've had women come into my office who were mourning the loss of the relationship with their lover, but more important, their sadness was because they had consented to the "no children" stipulation. These women felt they had made a significant, unalterable mistake. They don't have him, and they don't have children. Many have passed the child-bearing years.

Marriage

If your relationship is fairly new, you may feel confident that it will lead to marriage. As you put more time into the affair, the chance lessens that it will end in marriage. If you are having a long-term affair, you know the probability of marriage has greatly diminished. You may be waiting for certain events to pass, as he asked, at which point you expect him to leave her. If this happens two or more times, it is probably an indication that his intentions are not serious, and you may be headed for a long-term affair.

If you are a married woman having an affair, you need to be *very clear* about *why* you are involved with him. If you have made a mistake in choosing your husband, you do not want to repeat that error, and if it is a problem stemming from your childhood, you want to resolve that. The nature of the affair tells us that it may all be smoke and mirrors and different in the light of day. If you have children, they will definitely be affected by what occurs in your life. You must think very carefully, for the stakes are high.

Studies show the married woman is more likely to leave a marriage when she has an affair, but also has the most to lose. British sociologist Annette Lawson addresses this in her book *Adultery:* "I make it clear that adultery has always been a more serious problem for the adulterous married woman than for the adulterous married man, her punishment being greatly more severe than his."

Rather than jumping out of the fire and into the frying pan, I recommend you read the next chapters carefully and work on some of the exercises. You may decide at that point to work with a marriage counselor to understand yourself and your choices.

Emotional Well-Being

Is this affair, with all its feel-good qualities, a search for satisfaction of your emotional needs, or a distraction that keeps you from solving the problems from your childhood? If your childhood experience is intruding on your well-being now, and you are using the affair for comfort, you could be sacrificing your long-term emotional health by not dealing with the unhappy experiences from your past. Whether you marry him or not, your emotional well-being is vital. With it, you can better handle life's disappointments and traumas, and you can be the best that you can be as a person, wife, mother, and professional. You can trust your choice and judgment more when you understand your past.

Your Future Together

There are many affairs with a large age discrepancy between the couple. Even with the emphasis on exercise and good nutrition, as well as current pharmaceutical treatments for erectile dysfunction, there may be significant differences in the desires and capabilities of a twenty-five-year-old woman and a fifty-five-year-old man. And twenty years from now, when she is forty-five and he is seventy-five, the disparity will be even greater. It doesn't seem a consideration when you are young and in love, but in yet another fifteen years, that same woman will be sixty and he will be ninety!

While older women are still doing their thing, like singer Tina Turner and actresses Jacqueline Bisset and Sophia Loren, there are few male counterparts, apart from Clint Eastwood. If, for example, one of your life's goals is to travel, you will be able to do that at sixty, but I doubt you could travel with him very easily when he is ninety.

We hear more about older people marrying, but if they marry someone within their age range, they can have more reasonable expectations of each other. This is not age bias—it is looking ahead and reasonably assessing what life can be. If you are a younger woman involved in an affair with an older married man, you need to consider what you might have to sacrifice down the road—and seriously consider whether or not the scenario realistically fits in with your vision of your future.

Life on Hold

Many women are not just sacrificing their goals, their future, and their emotional well-being for the affair, but the everyday things that bring joy to life. You must clarify the relationship this affair has to your goals.

Women sacrifice friendships because of the affair and the secrecy required. They miss family events because they sit around waiting for their lover to call. Many women don't pursue activities they are interested in, like taking trips, signing up for classes, or joining groups—because of their lady-in-waiting status. And still others are so caught up with the secrecy, the excitement, and the danger of the affair that they miss the real danger—and that is not having a life apart from him.

Your Happiness

Twenty-two years ago in the very first group I ever led, I remember a woman asking how she could find happiness. The group discussed this and agreed that it was important to fill everyday life with activities and people you enjoy and to stop worrying about being happy. Are you able to do that?

When you free your thinking of the defense mechanisms we've talked about, there are questions to ask yourself that you need to answer truthfully. Do you see yourself being attracted to married men in previous relationships? Have you been attracted to older men in the past? If you have, you must consider the possibility that your relationships are following a pattern. This may be a conscious or unconscious process. An affair with a married man may indicate your desire for a loving father or mother figure, someone who will take good care of you. Or it may reflect your concern with issues of trust from childhood experiences. It could be that you seek out relationships that cannot work because on some level you do not want a committed relationship. It could be a desire to lose, not to win. What may basically attract you is his unavailability. Another possibility is that on some level you want to be in a powerless position. Your world of paradoxes leaves you powerless and with no control over your future. If you see a pattern of choosing lovers who are not free to marry you, then these are all possibilities for you to consider. To break such a pattern, you first need to be aware that it exists. Then you need to understand why such a need exists, and acquire the tools to help you change. In the next chapter, we will explore that in more detail.

Part III

The Affair

Chapter Six

The Stages of an Affair

*V*ery little in life remains static. People and relationships change. Sometimes they deepen, sometimes they gain in one respect and lose in another. In assessing your affair, a look at the changes will help you determine if it is developing in the way that you would like. Things seem to be going well in the beginning of relationships when there is that intoxication with the other person and a desire to please. If the relationship does not change and remains a physical one—the first leg of the triangle of love—with only passion and without emotional intimacy, it is not likely that it will deepen and that he will leave his wife for you.

As the relationship develops, *intimacy*, the second leg of the triangle, will also begin to grow. You will get to know each other better. Of course, intimacy is crucial to the development of true love. But it is at this point that reality sets in, enabling you to see more clearly who this person really is. You may discover some of the gold is tarnishing. Arguments can occur even though passion is still high. Passion is the positive reinforcement for the affair to continue.

However, as intimacy builds and if you discover that it is real gold and not tarnished, you will want the third part of the triangle: *commitment.* As you become more comfortable in the relationship, you begin to question your future together. He might at that point be torn between leaving his family and marrying you, or he may avoid the subject and even distance himself from you as he tries to sort things through. He may feel less comfortable in the relationship, unless he wants to be with you exclusively. Your reaction will probably be anger and you'll make more demands. A process begins that includes coming together and then coming apart. There is a reconciliation for a while and then the unresolved issue once again surfaces and the cycle is repeated.

It will repeat many times until you find an answer. The decision may be to end the relationship, to continue the affair, which could go on to become long term, or to marry. The following section will show the stages I have observed and the names that I think best describe them. The stages are not always sharply marked, but rather they meld, one into the other.

First Stage: Attraction

You meet and find to your delight that you are attracted to him and he returns the attention. At this time you may or may not know he is married, or you may deny that he could be married. Yet you may be finding yourself more and more attracted to him. As the relationship develops and is established, you feel as though you two are a couple. It may not be until you are more involved that you discover, or realize, that he is married, but this new information does not deter you. You may think about it for a while, but you tell yourself that he is not happy in his marriage. You make rationalizations to justify the relationship to yourself because his being married would be unacceptable: "If it weren't me, it would be someone else," or, "I can't hurt something that is already damaged."

The relationship is new, and you are dedicated to making your meetings with him the most wonderful part of his week, just as they are for you.

> *Edie:* "I didn't believe he was married, but some of the things he said and did made me wonder about him. On the other hand, I was lonely and I loved being with him. When I wasn't with him, I read and reread a note he gave me on my birthday. I knew he was just as attracted to me as I was to him. We just couldn't keep our hands off each other."

You continue with the affair because of this attraction, but most of all because you have entered the second stage of the affair.

Second Stage: The Honeymoon

This is the intoxicating, passionate stage of the affair. Power is an integral part of the affair and shifts throughout the stages. At this point, it seems that you have all the power due to the exciting and clandestine nature of the affair. You not only look forward to his calls and your meetings with him but you start obsessing about him. It is the secrecy that nurtures the obsession. When you are alone, you wonder what he is doing and if he is thinking of you. You start to plan your next meeting and think of what you want to do, say, and how it will feel to be with him.

In her autobiography, *My Life So Far,* Jane Fonda reveals an affair she had when there were problems in her marriage to Tom Hayden. She writes that her marriage improved during this period. Many women have seen this type of positive change in their marriage while involved in an affair. This is a response to the honeymoon stage of the affair when the passion is high and the woman's self-esteem rises. This feeling of exhilaration carries over to the marriage and for a while things seem to improve. It is temporary because the issues that led to the affair are still unresolved. For some, the affair is more like a distraction from the main event, the marriage.

Jane Fonda says that she ended the affair because she could not continue the deceit. However, the marriage continued as it was prior to the affair because the problems were not addressed, and these same problems plagued her next marriage because she had not yet faced her own demons.

If the affair continues past this stage, you start to build a life together while trying to ignore or forget he is married, but you sometimes find that hard to do. You begin to create rituals for your time together. It could be cocktails before dinner, watching a favorite television series, or cooking a Wednesday evening dinner together. You collect mementos from places you visit. You may take photos and create an album. You may start to buy things to use together for cooking, having sex, or going on picnics. You buy each other gifts. You may send him cards, if that is possible. You buy each other books. Sometimes, you devise a signal when you are in each other's presence but cannot communicate—to let him know you are thinking of him. You may wear a certain hat or piece of jewelry that has a meaning just for the two of you.

Edie: "I accidentally found out that he was married when I saw him and another woman at an Arts and Crafts show. I could tell from the expression on his face when he saw me and from the way he ignored me that she was his wife. It was confirmed the next day in our conversation. But I was so taken with him that I couldn't stop seeing him. I asked myself, 'What's worse, loneliness or seeing a married man?' I knew the answer, but I kept on. I didn't seem to have control. I always thought about the delight I felt whenever I was in his arms. My feelings overrode my common sense. But after a while I became more and more uneasy about it. I knew I wanted more and I kept bringing up the subject of our future."

The honeymoon stage can last awhile, until you slowly transition to the next stage, in which you not only hope that he will leave his wife, but you start to talk to him about it. At this point, the relationship begins to show instability as you transition into the next stage.

Third Stage: Disequilibrium

This is a turbulent time. There are arguments about your future together. Promises are made and broken, deadlines are set and passed, ultimatums issued and ignored, and no definitive decision is made. You become hurt, angry, and demanding. He tries to pacify you. You have many arguments, some of which result in breakups, but you are soon back together until the next spat. The arguments can be very intense and you say things you regret. All of this is a result of your frustration and feelings of powerlessness that are beginning to surface.

Edie: "We started to argue about it. He told me that he and his wife were opening a high-end Arts and Crafts gallery and that is why they were at the show. He said that this was just a bad time and I should be patient. After a few more conversations like that I got the message. At first I started a whole beauty routine—facials, manicures, pedicures—until I realized it wasn't about being beautiful. I just was not the love of his life and I couldn't do anything about it."

There is not as much arguing if he experiences the affair as a romantic love affair. He will be considering a major life decision, and he will be torn between you and his family. He may leave his wife and marry you, or he may decide to end the affair. Such a decision may not have so much to do with you, but with his sense of duty or moral convictions. This is a different process than setting deadlines that come and go. It is likely that if he is struggling with a decision because he considers it a romantic love affair, he will be sharing this process with you. This process is building the third side of the triangle: commitment.

This is a very difficult time for the married woman having an affair with a married man. For her, the affair is riskier than for the single woman. She could obtain a divorce and then hope her lover will do the same. She feels she must trust him to marry her if she leaves her husband. Statistics are against this happening.

> *Donna:* "I told him he would have to do it first. People get cold feet, and where would I be if he didn't go through with his divorce?"

This is a critical stage and I will have more to say about it in the following section entitled "Distancer and Pursuer."

Fourth Stage: An Answer

At this point, an ending to the search for an answer occurs. If he really had no serious intentions, he will end the affair because of the tension and problems it is causing him. He may feel he cannot cope with your anger or could be concerned you may tell his wife of the affair. The safe haven may feel more like a web of entanglements he doesn't want.

> *Edie:* "So I ended it and I feel really bad, really bad and that's why I'm here for therapy. I want a happy life and it's not going that way. Happy on Tuesday and Thursday nights just isn't doing it for me."

Like Edie, you may end it because you realize he is not serious. The affair can either end with an argument, or just wind down. Or you could go on with the affair with the understanding that he will not marry you.

The Lady-in-Waiting

Many of the things you want to happen are beyond your control. If you are waiting for an answer from your lover, then essentially he determines what your future will be. You are a modern lady-in-waiting, while his wife, the queen, occupies the position you want and the king has all the power. His wife has more power than you have, but she, too, is being cheated of the relationship she wants.

Psychiatrist Richard Tuch, in his book *The Single Woman–Married Man Syndrome*, says of the single woman having the affair, "He has two women, she has half a man."

And it seems the lady-in-waiting cannot count on that half a man when she wants indications from him that he is serious. She is asking for a commitment, but he is not forthcoming with one. It is obvious he has the power. She has handed over control of her destiny to him. When things you want are on hold and you cannot change the situation, then you are without power in that relationship.

The dynamics of the affair are influenced by which one has the power. He has had the power in part because secrecy dictates the way you live. This is seen in the dance of pursuer and distancer that the couple engages in.

Distancer and Pursuer

A period of pursuing and distancing is seen in the third stage of the affair, characterized by breakups and reconciliations. The power shifts back and forth. Psychiatrist Thomas Fogarty describes a movement between two people in a relationship who want closeness, but instead manage to keep themselves at a distance from each other by dancing between two points.

We can see this happening in affairs. It is the "dance" of pursuing and distancing. The woman is usually the pursuer because she wants intimacy. She becomes anxious when she thinks he is pulling away or distancing, so she pursues him. He then becomes anxious over her pursuit and moves further away. He feels smothered by intimacy. Eventually, the pursuer stops pursuing and the distancer comes back to her because it feels safer.

This dance is repeated, but will not be resolved until the individuals identify the real issue: why they cannot deal with their anxiety while maintaining contact with each other. The pursuer's issue is fear of abandonment and the distancer's issue is fear of intimacy.

Joline: "I feel so alone when he doesn't call. Is it asking too much of him to pick up the phone?"

Bob: "I feel smothered. What do I have to do to let her know I care?"

Joline and Bob are both issuing messages of powerlessness and can easily fall into the roles of pursuer and distancer. They could become like Page and Gary, who are actively doing this dance.

Page is a single, thirty-two-year-old woman who lives in Los Angeles and is a pharmaceutical company representative. All her adult life she has striven to be an independent woman. And she is just that in her career. She is proud of her work record and the excellent salary she makes. But she has not been able to achieve that independence in her relationships, even though that is a conscious goal. Page had difficulties maintaining relationships and started working with a therapist to understand why that was so. Although Page got along with her father, she resented his detachment from her mother. She felt her mother was a "doormat" who put up with poor treatment from her father. Page was aware that her family life had something to do with her difficulty in maintaining relationships, but could not really understand how it did.

Page: "It was thrilling to be so loved by Gary. He only had eyes for me. I loved that because my father had eyes for every woman he saw.

"I felt my bad luck with men was changing when I met Gary. All my other relationships fell apart. So all my happiness was pinned on him. We met at a Christmas party. He is a building contractor for a large firm and he travels a lot. It is something like my own job in a way because I drive all around the city going from one doctor's office to another.

"He started asking me out for dinner. He never hid the fact that he was married. I thought of him as someone to have dinner with. That was all, but I really fell for him.

"When I started talking about wanting more time, he became quiet. I know now that I have a pattern of going after someone in an inappropriate way. I think it was because I did not want anyone to take advantage of me. No way was I going to be a doormat. I mean, if I'm sleeping with someone, doesn't he owe me something more besides dinner?

"So I started calling him at the office and on his cell phone over and over again when I knew he was on the road. Finally, he told me I couldn't bug him like that and to cool it if we were to stay together.

"I agreed, but it was never the same after that. I kept trying in nice ways to change things. I bought us tickets for sports events. If I didn't hear from him for a while, I called and left messages. When he didn't return messages, I started going to his office to see if his car was there and waiting a while for him to come out of the building. One day he came out and told me that it was over. He told me that if I came to his office once more he would get a restraining order.

"I was stunned. I am not a stalker. I don't know what happened to me. I stopped calling and I am trying to forget about him. It's been five weeks. He left a message for me on my answering machine two days ago, and that is why I am here. I was so relieved to hear his voice. I want to call him, but maybe I shouldn't."

Gary distanced himself from Page because she wanted more intimacy than he could tolerate. When this happened, Page panicked because she felt abandoned. She then pursued him. When she stopped pursuing, Gary relaxed and he stopped distancing. Soon Page will want more intimacy and so their dance will continue.

Page is now interested in exploring her family background to understand the role that abandonment has played in her life and why she picks men who fear intimacy. Gary would also be wise to find the answer to his reaction to intimacy.

Shifts in Feelings of Self-Esteem

As we have noted, in the beginning of the affair, self-esteem increases for both and becomes a positive reinforcement to continue seeing each other.

Iris: "Just being with him made my life wonderful. I became another person—happy, talkative, and in love. When he leaves, I sink inside. It is usually the thought of seeing him again that helps me make it through the in-between time."

Individuals want to continue doing things that make them feel good, but soon time becomes a factor in this equation. At about the time when there is a shift in power, there is an accompanying shift in self-esteem. This happens when you start to wonder about your future with him and he becomes uncomfortable with that. There is a decline in how the affair makes you feel. When you are with him, the good feelings return. But they may not last long, because your desire to be with him permanently is presenting a problem for him. So you continue to pursue him, wanting to get back the power and self-esteem that you are losing. Before you can be empowered, you need to understand what rights you have.

Personal Rights

You do not have the right to her husband unless she gives it to you or he divorces her. But you do have the right to be treated respectfully and honestly by your lover. Your time is not being respected when he asks you to wait until he can manage to fit you into his schedule. Essentially, you have given him control over the direction of your life. The nature of the affair is that you are at his mercy and he makes the rules.

In any situation of powerlessness, you must know who has the power and decide on your strategy, because the only person you can change is yourself. Monica Lewinsky is an example of a young woman who didn't understand power. She was having an affair with the most powerful man in the free world, and she had no power in this relationship. She was unable to recognize that she could not possibly have it because of the circumstances of the affair.

A man doesn't have to be president of the United States of America to have such power. Many men having affairs are in a position of control in the relationship, and until the woman recognizes this and learns what she can do about it, she is without power.

Who Has the Power?

If you are not certain about who has the power in your affair, answer these questions. Answer "yes" to any question that describes the way you feel or behave.

1. Your needs go unmet because his take priority.
2. You frequently give up plans to do something you want so that you can be with him.
3. You want to include him in important events in your life, but you know he will not attend.
4. When you have needed him for emotional comfort, he could not be with you because of his family's needs.
5. You are unable to tell your family or friends about him except in a vague way.
6. You are frightened he will leave if you say what you want.
7. You feel you must maintain an aura of the beautiful "together" lover or he will lose interest.
8. If he treats you poorly, you are afraid to speak up because he may see you as he sees his wife.
9. He often vetoes your suggestions about where you would like to go or what you would like to do.
10. Your behavior is often influenced by the fear that he will leave you.
11. If you were to become ill or incapacitated in any way, you fear he would not be there for you.
12. Your self-esteem is tied to his opinion of you.
13. You feel you have no choice in your future.
14. He says your relationship is over only to give you clues that he wants it to go on.
15. He avoids or puts off discussions concerning your future together.
16. You have declined career or educational opportunities because you want to be near him.

If you have answered yes to even one statement, you need to think very carefully about your position of powerlessness in this relationship. When you have no power, you cannot make the decisions that determine your future together. However, you *do* have the power to determine your own individual future.

Three Perspectives

As we have seen, affairs tend to run a course, but there are some variations. The affair can be different depending on whether the woman is single or married.

The Single Woman

The American public witnessed an affair between a married man and a young woman who hoped her lover would someday leave his wife and marry her. That woman is Monica Lewinsky. We can learn from both Special Counsel Kenneth Starr's report and Andrew Morton's biography of Monica Lewinsky, *Monica's Story.* Because we are familiar with Monica's story from the barrage of news coverage, it is an excellent example. We will see the reasons and the stages of the affair between a married man and a single woman. We benefit from understanding the woman before the affair, during, and after. Of course, not all will apply to you, but some will.

Low self-esteem

Monica was always, as one of her friends described her, a "chubette," which made life difficult for her at Beverly Hills High School. Although she was a good student, smart, witty, and pretty, she grew up thinking that she was undesirable and that anyone who paid attention to her did so out of pity, or because there was no one else around. She used food for comfort in relation to the stresses of her life, including the time of her White House internship and throughout the ordeal that resulted from Kenneth Starr's investigation of President Clinton. Monica said that the affairs she had made her feel desired and increased her self-esteem.

The flattering words that men spoke to Monica stayed with her, and she found she could go over and over them when she was alone. This was reflected in a temporary increase in her self-esteem that reinforced her desire to continue the affairs.

Certainly not everyone having an affair with a married man has low self-esteem. The women described by Laurel Richardson in *The New Other Woman*, for example, felt generally good about their accomplishments in life. These women found the positive feedback from their lover improved their self-esteem even more.

Cold and distant father

Monica's father has been characterized as cold and distant. As a child she always hoped that something would happen to make him care about her more than she believed he did. She recalled that when her mother filed for divorce, citing her husband's infidelity with a nurse, Monica was thirteen. Her mother chose to tell Monica and her younger brother, Michael, about the divorce on an outing to the Hamburger Hamlet restaurant. She was shocked when the children were devastated by the news. Michael started crying and Monica ran to the restroom to be sick. Monica was so angry at her father that she was estranged from him during her teenage years. Their relationship improved later, and he was very supportive during Monica's ordeal with the Starr investigation.

The men she picked

Three of the men Monica had affairs with were older, and all were poor-risk partners. Two of the men were married. Not one was an appropriate choice for a young single woman.

When Monica was in high school, she met Andy Bleiler, a twenty-five-year-old drama technician who had a reputation for flirting with the high school students. It was common knowledge during this time that Bleiler was engaged to be married. He and Monica began their flirtation, which led to an affair in 1991. Bleiler took Monica to motels when she was a high school student. During this time, he married, and as Morton points out, Monica "lost her virginity to a man whose wife recently became pregnant." The Lewinsky family did not report Bleiler's predatory behavior to school authorities. Monica continued her affair with him off and on through college and during the time she worked at the White House.

President Clinton was twice Monica's age when they had their affair. While at the Pentagon, she had another affair with a man she met there. She not only continued the pattern of picking a father figure, but once again she picked a poor-risk partner as well. This man, whom Monica does not identify but refers to as Thomas, was not married and is described as a "craggy-faced, older man." As the affair was ending, Monica found herself pregnant. When she told Thomas, he told her that he was involved with another woman and he would not help her pay for the abortion.

Affairs were the focus of her life

The affairs with the president and Bleiler became the focus of Monica's life. She did not seek the White House internship because of interest in government and politics, but at the suggestion of her mother and her aunt, who were concerned about the inappropriate relationship with Bleiler. They thought a change of scene would help. It did not. The affair with Bleiler continued wherever she lived—California, Oregon, Washington, D.C. Monica was unable to give up the affair.

Like other women involved in an affair, Monica obsessed over it. Monica told Morton of staying at home at nights and on weekends with the hopes that the president might call. She, however, was not discreet about it. She told her family and friends. This, we know, was to come back to haunt her at the hands of Linda Tripp.

Role of the wife

Monica did not seem to concern herself with how the affairs affected the wives of these men. She seemed focused only on the affair. In fact, she came to know Bleiler's wife, and even baby-sat for them. She was, however, aware of Hillary Rodham Clinton's daily schedule, and she became angry when she saw reports on TV of the president and the First Lady dancing on the beach while on vacation.

Repeated breakups and reconciliations

The relationships with both the president and Bleiler developed into a series of breakups and reconciliations. Monica became angry and demanding over what she saw as slights. She wanted more from the relationships than they were willing to give. She told the Starr investigators that when the president had an appointment in the Oval Office or played golf instead of seeing her, she went "ballistic." One of his appointments was with Eleanor Mondale, whom Monica saw as competition, accusing him of having an affair with her. The president told her at one point, "If I had known what kind of person you were, I wouldn't have gotten involved with you." Another time, when she made veiled threats of disclosure, he told her it was "illegal to threaten the president."

Fantasy

Monica testified in the Kenneth Starr investigation that she believed the president was "her soul mate" and that he told her "he might be alone in three years." She said, "I left that day just sort of stunned, for I knew he was in love with me."

What started out as flirting and sexual playfulness with a married man ended up—for her—as a romantic love affair. Monica had ten sexual contacts with the president over a twenty month period. He called her at her apartment and they often spent long hours on the phone, including having phone sex. Looking at it from her viewpoint, it is not difficult to understand how a young woman could hope that one day he would be free to marry her.

Monica did not recognize important factors in her situation, such as the danger to her reputation, the family to whom the president was devoted, the position he held, and the enormity of the possible political repercussions if the affair were to be revealed. Nor did she recognize that she had virtually no power in the relationship, and that she lost the little she had as she started to ask for more of his attention. Her background and her needs helped place her there. She was in a no-win situation and a pawn in the midst of a political "dirty war" against the president.

It was only later, when she was able to get some distance from the affair, that she understood the role of power in an affair. She told Morton, "I realize that I put myself in a situation where I had no control. . . . He had control over the relationship."

Monica's situation illustrates the basic dynamics of an affair between a married man and a single woman, even though hers was a more complicated situation than most single women or married women face. Most women having an affair will not have to face a grand jury, a special investigator, the fear of prosecution, and worry about time in prison. Situations do differ. The married woman still goes through the same stages, but there are other considerations because of her marital status.

The Married Woman

The married woman must also be concerned with the type of man she picks, the fluctuation in power and self-esteem, the breakups and reconciliations, and the obsession with the affair. But she must keep her emotions under control at home so that she does not give away her secret. If she is feeling happy and showing any display of this emotion, it will bewilder her husband, who may not see any justification for it and start to wonder about it. If she is depressed or angry over the way the affair is going, she must keep those emotions under control as well. This is not easy to do. She must also use care not to take out any frustrations from the affair on her children.

Her time is pretty much accounted for, and any absences or disruptions in her schedule might be noticed. Too many may signal a trend to an observant husband. She is on guard not to accidentally call her husband by her lover's name or if her lover is a family friend, not to talk about him too frequently. She cannot easily spend her time waiting for him to call because she must continue with her family life. She must make plans with her husband, their friends, their families, and their children. Her time for the affair is more limited and does not allow for the flexibility that the single woman has.

It is not easy for the married woman to accept gifts, because they must be explained if noticed by her husband or family. The manner in which she sends her lover gifts also requires special care so that there are no telltale signs that could be detected. For those gifts that she does accept, she must have a plausible explanation, and one that she can remember. The same holds true for notes and cards he might send her. They must be read, remembered, and destroyed. To hide them risks detection. Phone calls can easily be detected by checking phone bills. She must be aware of other technological footprints left on caller ID, e-mails, and computer files. Spyware on computers is a very sophisticated trap. If she is away on an outing with him, she must remember not to use her charge card, because she may have to explain why she was where she was that day.

If the married woman has children, she must always consider them in her planning. She must be certain that they are not present at any of their meetings or overhear telephone conversations. She must be careful about neighbors and coworkers who may come to their own conclusions about what seems like a closer than normal relationship between the two.

The married woman must have some idea of how she will extricate herself from her marriage to marry her lover if he should ask. She has the most to lose of the three in the marital triangle. He must want to marry her and she must determine if he is being truthful. To be jilted when you leave your marriage, regardless of how unhappy you may be in it, is a major jolt to your emotional system with enormous repercussions in your life. Going from married woman to single mom is an extremely stressful transition. Married women having an affair need to have a broader perspective that includes her children, her husband, and what is happening in her marriage.

Almost everyone has seen, read, or heard reports that an affair will spice up a marriage, but is this true? Yes, it might temporarily, due to the rise in self-esteem when someone is enthralled with you, and yes, the planning of clandestine meetings makes life appear exciting. This glow will carry over to your marriage, but the improvement will decrease when the affair enters the disequilibruium stage and your attitude changes from excitement to worry and concern. You may also find yourself unable to continue living a lie, angry over your lady-in-waiting status and his inability to give support when you feel you are in need of it.

Some women find that the triangular aspect of the affair can keep them from achieving intimacy with either husband or lover. For those who cannot tolerate intimacy, the relief that is found from this can carry over to the marriage. So once again, understanding your own needs will help you find out why the affair improves your marriage. But remember, the situation is more than likely temporary, and getting to the reasons is the way to improve the marriage and your life.

When Bryna first came to see me she only wanted to sort out her concerns about her affair with Charlie. She did not want to explore the whole picture. Bryna told me she found Charlie to be attractive and attentive. She knew he was married, just as she was. In fact, she knew who his wife was because she was a popular figure in the town of Columbia, Maryland, where they lived.

> "I was just swept off my feet. I was feeling so low and he was just so charming and adorable. I know I was vulnerable at that time. I still am for that matter. Charlie took my mind off my problems.

"There is a possibility that Jake and I may have to sell our house or take a second mortgage. He and his brother started a business online and that is now doing poorly. Jake moonlights designing Web sites to make ends meet, but he is depressed. He is so serious. I mean, it isn't the end of the world. Jake won't talk to me and rebuffs any suggestion I make.

"Deep down I am very frightened. I'd rather be with my lover. My husband is looking pretty bad next to him. I know that sounds terrible, but I am being honest."

We can see the losses Bryna is trying to cope with. She is living with a depressed husband and views her future as bleak. Jake will not discuss the situation with her. Along comes Charlie and she has excitement and a distraction from her own fears. She tries to cope with her problems by minimizing when she says that it isn't the end of the world.

"Charlie and I hardly have any time together. We meet at lunch because we work in the same office complex and sometimes we just go for a walk in the park. We sometimes go to a nearby motel when we think we can get away with it at work. There are times we say we are working late and go to a bar or to the motel. It is very hard to do because I am juggling the care of a toddler and a three-year-old, as well as my job, and Jake's schedule. But it is worth it.

"Charlie's wife, Dottie, has little time for him. She is very busy with her social activities. I know, because I read about her and see that she attends many events. Charlie says she is bossy and demanding and he is unhappy in the marriage. She has just about destroyed his self-esteem, but I am restoring it. It makes me feel good because I can help him even if I can't help Jake.

"A turning point came in my feelings about Charlie last winter when his wife went on her annual woman's retreat in Annapolis. We took his little girl and my two boys to a magic show for toddlers and kindergarten children in Baltimore. We planned it in advance and bought tickets so that we could sit together. The children, of course, were too young to understand. And we had decided to tell our spouses that we ran into someone from work while we were at the magic show. So we felt safe.

"We each took a seat on the end with the kids in between. It seemed wonderful. We loved it and I could picture myself with Charlie like this with our children. It was then that I knew I wanted to marry him. I proposed a few trips on the weekend, but we can never find a way to do it. He talks about our future together, but I can't pin him down. I don't think he feels the same excitement for me as I do for him. Maybe it is one-sided and I really don't appeal to him. I don't sleep well at night. I want him to say something. I can't live with my depressed husband and I want to know Charlie's intentions."

Bryna is at the start of the disequilibrium stage where she is beginning to feel the shift in power in the relationship and a slip in her self-esteem. Until recently, the affair was a distraction from her husband's depression and the serious financial problems in her marriage. She is focusing on the affair and ignoring the repercussions from Jake's psychological state.

After only a few sessions Bryna came to see me in a terrible state. Charlie had told her that he was leaving Dottie, but he was not going to marry her. He just wanted to be alone and get his life in order.

"I pleaded with him. I begged, but he said that this is what he had to do and he gave me that line that it wasn't me, it was him. He was unhappy in his marriage and I showed him that it was possible to be happy again. I can't believe this and I can't understand it."

I was able to help Bryna understand what had happened. Charlie's affair with Bryna was more about him leaving his wife than about marrying her. In our book *Surviving Infidelity*, Gloria Harris and I identify this type of affair as the Exit Affair. Some men who want to leave a marriage have an affair as a way of testing out their abilities to attract new partners and perform sexually with another woman. Others use the affair as a way to transition into single life by taking a lover who will become a source of support at a difficult time. Still others use an affair as a way to create a crisis in the marriage that will lead to counseling, so the wife will get professional support as he departs.

The Exit Affair is a cruel and self-centered attempt at a solution to a person's problems.

Bryna was in a great deal of pain after Charlie's disclosure. She felt betrayed and used. She spent her time in therapy sorting through her affair and the issues that had developed in her marriage—which is the first step toward resolution and healing for the married woman.

The Older Married Woman

Different developmental issues affect why an older woman has an affair in the first place, as well as how that affair plays out.

Jane is such a woman. This is what she told her support group:

"Bill and I have been married for thirty-nine years. We started a family when we were very young. I started out as a traditional mom, like my mother. Bill was an engineer and very involved with his work.

"I was very influenced by the Women's Movement, but torn because I wanted to be home with my kids. So I went back to college while my children were in school and got my degree as a city planner. I couldn't find a part-time job, so I became a travel agent.

"There are lots of perks for travel agents, but Bill didn't want to take any trips. In fact, he didn't want to do much of anything. I realized that we were different. He thought I was 'too emotional,' and I thought he was 'cold.'

"About five years ago, I started working for a hotel chain. I basically put my city planning skills and travel business together, and lucked out on the greatest job I could ever imagine. I'm part of a team that scouts locations for new sites for a big hotel chain.

"I have been having an affair with a guy on this team named Mike for four of the five years that we have worked together. I'm fifty-seven, and he is sixty-four. He will retire in another year, and he and his wife will relocate to a retirement village in Florida.

"I know he loves me. I can't face life with Bill. Mike makes it tolerable. I know as you get older there are many losses. Time is going by so quickly. I feel I have only come alive these last five years with Mike."

Jane's situation shows how the developmental stages of life and social events shape our lives, and how they can affect a marriage. The passing years also give her a sense of urgency that some younger women may not have. Jane feels like she placed her life on hold in the past, and now fears she will once again find herself doing the same thing, only now facing the problems of growing older. She wants to enjoy her life before it is too late.

This chapter opened with, "Very little in life remains static. People and relationships change." We have reviewed how the affair changes and goes through stages. There is still another piece in the puzzle of the affair: the meshing of each person's background and how they come together and culminate in an affair. In the next chapter we will look at how family dynamics are played out in affairs.

Chapter Seven

Assessing Your Affair

*C*arol is in Jimmy's arms and sighs, "It is so wonderful, just the two of us." She is not alone in these thoughts and feelings. These are the words and feelings of most lovers, but actually, Carol is not completely accurate. When lovers are in bed together, or anywhere else for that matter, they feel it is just the two of them. But there are others there, maybe not physically, but psychologically present and exerting great influence.

In reality, our family background helps to determine our personality and our behavior to a significant degree. There are other determinants as well—our genetic makeup, life experiences, and social environment. If we are uncomfortable with our behavior and realize we are having difficulties in our relationships, it is helpful to examine the influences of the past and learn new skills to effect change.

Many psychologists and therapists recognize the importance of doing just this. In his book *Forgive Your Parents, Heal Yourself*, Dr. Barry Grosskopf writes, "When parents act in harmful ways toward their children, it is a sign that something harmful has happened to them." As children we watch and copy how our parents solve their problems, and our decisions in life are often based on what we have observed. We also react to the family atmosphere. As children we may not know the cause of any tension, but we sense it when something is wrong. Yet, others do not know that anything is amiss and regard this as "normal" family interactions. You can see that the family is very important in who we are and what choices we make.

This chapter will help you look at the past generations and see their relevance to affairs. We start with a look back at the family: parents and siblings are known as our family-of-origin.

The Family-of-Origin

The late Dr. Murray Bowen, founder of the Georgetown Family Center, developed the Bowen Family System Theory that explains the family emotional system. It is an intergenerational view of the family. We will look at a part of his theory to help us understand affairs.

The cornerstone of this theory is "differentiation," which means the ability to be who you are, or "self-defined," in the presence of pressure from others. "Well-differentiated" individuals are able to be different, meaning they can make decisions without being coerced into doing something against their own core beliefs to please another person. People exist on a continuum of poorly to well differentiated. When faced with a problem situation, the well-differentiated person thinks it through by taking into account the concerns of others, but makes the decision based on reason and not solely on emotions or coercion by another. By contrast, a person who makes a decision based only on emotions or coercion is "poorly differentiated." In this book, I use the term "differentiation" because it is used in the theory, but "emotional maturity" may be substituted.

Differentiation is marked by the degree to which people can separate their "thinking" from their "feelings." When individuals react automatically to a high-anxiety situation without thinking the situation through, they are said to be "emotionally reactive." This can be thought of as "shooting from the hip." The more differentiated an individual is, the better he or she can manage anxiety.

The inability to stay differentiated in situations of high anxiety is evident in certain behaviors, such as emotional cutoff, engaging in constant conflict, or triangling. Poorly differentiated individuals can also feed off one another's anxiety, creating an escalating spiral of reactive behavior. You may have had such an experience when a friend or relative called to tell you about a troubling situation, and soon you, too, were sharing that person's anxiety.

For change to occur in situations of high anxiety, the individual must first reduce emotional reactivity. When you are calm, you can be more objective. This is one of the goals of this book—to help you reduce your emotional reactivity so that you can understand the facts and think through your situation to a satisfactory resolution.

Someone who lives her life to please another is "fused" with that person; that is, she finds that emotionally she cannot allow herself to be different. So she is not self-defined. Self-definition is achieved by taking an "I position." Dr. Peter Titelman, in *Clinical Applications of Bowen Family Systems Theory*, writes, "They [I positions] are a serious reflection of important principles of living." They are used judiciously when important personal principles cannot be compromised. This differs from "I" statements, which are statements of preference used in everyday communication; for example, "I would like you to turn down the television volume."

An example of a person who is poorly differentiated is the woman who marries someone she doesn't love because of the anxiety she experiences from family pressure to marry. Someone in such a predicament might try to escape the pressure by cutting off contact with the family. It is only by taking a stand for oneself that emotional maturity or differentiation can be gained, such as in the "I position." Rather than taking an "I position," she might distance herself from the source of her coercion by moving to the other side of the country, or by not speaking to her parents, but she is just as fused as the woman who acquiesces. This process of distancing to gain relief from external pressure is called "emotional cutoff."

One of the concepts of Bowen Theory is the creation of triangles in relationships. When a relationship is unstable for whatever reason, one partner may attempt to stabilize it by forming a triangle. This third leg of the triangle is used to alleviate some of the anxiety. It can be many things: drugs, work, alcohol, projecting problems onto a child—or having an affair. It may reduce the anxiety, but it is only a temporary solution.

According to San Diego marriage and family therapist Sally LeBoy, "The danger for couples who triangle in a third party is that the underlying causes of the couple's problem go unexamined. The triangle could include a child, the family-of-origin, or an affair. While triangles can reduce conflict or stress, they never lead to greater understanding or growth. Detouring conflict onto a third party means that the underlying problem persists, sometimes over many generations."

In *My Life* by former President Bill Clinton, he relates his affair with Monica Lewinsky to the emotional issues in his own life. He writes about the weekly counseling sessions he and Hillary had after his affair. "For the first time in my life I actually talked openly about feelings, experiences, and opinions about life, love, and the nature of relationships.

I didn't like everything I learned about myself or my past, and it pained me to face the fact that my childhood and the life I'd led since growing up have made some things difficult for me that seemed to come more naturally to other people."

Affairs involve sex, but they are about much more. When individuals are able to look more deeply into their feelings and needs, they can find the answer to their search. Often this means looking back into childhood.

Jane Fonda, in her book *My Life So Far,* writes, "There are, of course, those lucky few who grew up in homes, where the child saw her parents work out their differences in a loving and respectful way; where the parents when they were there, were really, wholly, fully there." Fonda was in many ways a strong and independent woman. However, she lived with a great deal of emotional pain in her life. Her three marriages ended in divorce, her husbands cheated on her, and she herself had an affair. She repeatedly put herself in situations that made her uncomfortable or that she regretted because her goal was to please others. This was done even at the sacrifice of her feelings of self-worth. Like Gloria Vanderbilt, as well as many other women, Jane Fonda had been searching for love, caring, and positive regard from parents who were unable to give it or express it, even though their job as parents was to provide it. The futile search for relief from pain through affairs or marriages that are not working will not yield an answer. The problem, and the search for an answer, will more than likely be passed on to the next generation—or even the generation that follows.

Genogram

A useful tool to help us understand families and how they deal with problems is called a "genogram." This is a family tree that shows the history of the family including important events, significant emotional problems, and the way in which the family handles them. Symbols are used to represent each family member and how they relate to one another.

There are many benefits of making a genogram, and almost everyone I have counseled likes to see this map depicting their family life. It gives information that people seem to overlook. No one is asked to delve into the unconscious—only to observe events and family reactions to them. While working on a genogram, people begin to understand how they find themselves in their present situation. Some tell me they feel they were almost programmed to act as they have. This understanding usually reduces anger and guilt, and replaces them with a thoughtful process that can result in a change of behavior.

Following is a history of a family that is coping with the issue of infidelity. You will see how information from the past and current information are important to understanding what is happening. This is true for all three people in the triangle.

The Story of Al, Sandy, and Jodi

The Situation

Al is a forty-seven-year-old philosophy professor at a New England college who has just recently ended an affair of four months with Jodi, his graduate student. Jodi is twenty-five years old and employed full-time as an elementary school teacher. Jodi is very angry and hurt because Al ended their affair.

Al's wife, Sandy, is thirty-six years old and a virologist who will be applying for tenure at the same college. She had taken on a field assignment in Africa for six months to support her application for tenure. While Sandy was in Africa, Al had an affair with Jodi that he ended shortly before his wife's return. Sandy found out about Al's infidelity through a phone call from Jodi, who has called Al's home many times. She has begun to argue with both Al and Sandy. Jodi is very emotionally reactive. We understand her anger. She now threatens a sexual harassment case. Sandy is outraged. Additionally, she and Al have been arguing about his infidelity.

Al and Sandy have been married for eighteen years and have a daughter, Rae, who is seventeen years old and is a senior in high school. Rae has a serious relationship with John, another senior, and they plan to attend the same college.

Al's Family History

Al has had no previous history of infidelity. His father is dead and his mother lives nearby. His mother had a difficult relationship with her husband. She resented his job that took him "on the road" and away from the family. She came from a large family, in which she, as the eldest of six children was made responsible for helping her mother with housecleaning and child care. She felt as though she skipped her childhood and was once again in the same position in her own family. Al's mother in turn made him, as the oldest, responsible for many of the same duties. His father was not there much so he was not available as a role model. His mother was a hard taskmistress. She was an angry woman, and because of it, Al was under much criticism. However, he became a person who knew how to take care of others and take charge.

Sandy's Family History

Sandy's father died when she was ten years old. Her mother, who had been a stay-at-home mom, then went to work outside of the home and Sandy was left to be supervised by her older brother. When Al and Sandy met, he was accustomed to being a caretaker to girls, and to Sandy he seemed a replacement for the father she had lost when she was so young. They had one daughter with whom Al was close and whose best interests were always foremost on his mind. He and Sandy always felt they had a good marriage and were happy together.

Jodi's Family History

Jodi is an only child. She has not seen her father since her parents divorced when she was eleven, but she remembers him well because he physically abused her mother and verbally abused Jodi. After the divorce, her mother had a series of love affairs. Two of the men lived with them for a few years. When her mother died two years ago, Jodi was heartbroken. She went back to school, this time as a graduate student. She tried to compensate for the pain of her childhood by being a good student. She took courses in the evening twice a week with Al. He was a very supportive teacher, working with students after hours.

Family System's View

When Sandy went to Africa, it was the first time Al could remember when he had no one to care for. He was lonely, but more than that, his daughter spent much of her time with her boyfriend. Al felt very alone and saw himself as useless. As he put it, he felt like "a man without a cause." Soon Jodi became his new cause. Jodi had spent her life looking for what had always eluded her—a father. She found caring and understanding from Al. However, in Al's attempt to find another person to care for, and thus to reduce his anxiety, what he actually did was abusive to Jodi.

Although Jodi wished that Sandy would stay in Africa, she felt Sandy, like her father, had deserted the family. When Al ended the affair with Jodi, she re-experienced the abandonment by her father.

How can we explain this affair when Sandy and Al considered themselves to be happily married? Each had looked to the other to satisfy unmet needs from childhood, and for a long while it worked. It was only when Sandy went to Africa, and their daughter was no longer dependent upon Al, that his need surfaced to feel good about himself by caring for others. When Jodi appeared, he once again had his cause. None of us has a crystal ball, but we wonder, if Sandy had not gone to Africa, would Al have continued his life as a faithful husband? Maybe that would have happened, because he could carry on as he had been and not look too closely at his needs stemming from his childhood. By the same token, we can ask if Jodi, with her complementary needs, had not come into Al's life at that time, would Al have looked elsewhere for an affair or would he have waited out Sandy's return even though he felt anxious?

We have looked at the past stressors in the lives of the couple and the lover, but another source of information that will help us evaluate the affair are the stressors anyone in the marital triangle has experienced the year or so before the affair. So it is advisable to look closely at that period.

Current Stressors

In this situation we see the stressors clearly:

1. For Al, it was his wife's absence and his daughter's growing independence and preoccupation with her boyfriend.
2. For Jodi, it was her mother's death.
3. For Sandy, it was her separation from Al and Rae, and adjustment to Africa.

These events alone were stressful, but coupled with the issues from each individual's family-of-origin, it made them more vulnerable. Discovery of the affair became an additional stressor for the family.

Ida's Story

The following story will show how a family in which there is infidelity and emotional cutoff results in one child carrying the pain of the family.

The Situation

Ida, a sixty-nine-year-old woman, came to see me with a problem that at first seemed to have no relation to affairs.

> "My heart is broken over my relationship with my son, David. He is a grown man and he doesn't ever call. He was also angry with his father when his father was alive. I don't know why he acts like this. I am not well and I need help from him. He gives it grudgingly when I ask, but he never volunteers. His older brother, Jacob, gladly helps, but I don't want to always call on him. It came to a head for me last weekend when David came to help me with some legal forms and I asked him if he loved me. I know his brother does and I couldn't stand it any longer, so I asked. He looked at me and said nothing. Then he walked out. I cried and cried, and my brother suggested I talk to someone."

The first red flag that went up for me is the difference between the attitudes of the brothers. I asked her to work on a family history with me to see if we could uncover this mystery.

Family History

This is the story that Ida told me in bits and pieces through our conversations until it made sense to both of us.

Sam and I were married a few years when our first son, Jacob, was born, and five years later David was born. Sam was not an easy man to live with, but I tried my best. One day, Sam told me he wanted a divorce and that he was in love with another woman. I cried and cried. What was I to do? I had only a high school education. I never worked. It was a different time. Now girls are smart, they know how to take care of themselves. I called Sam's older brother, who hit the ceiling and immediately drove from San Francisco down to the Valley and he read Sam the riot act. He told him, "You're a family man. You have responsibilities, kids, and a wife, so shape up. You don't want to be like Pop."

What did he mean, "like Pop"?

Oh, years ago his father had an affair. The family won't talk about it, but I know it happened. But that did the trick. Sam gave up his affair and we tried to get back to where we were.

Did you?

Well, he bought me a mink coat and I tried very hard to look good all the time.

And what about the children?

They didn't know about any of this and they still don't.

And their relationship with their father?

Sam adored Jacob.

And how did he feel about David?

They never got on. Actually, David was always afraid of Sam and Sam was not warm to him.

What year was David born?

1985.

How did Sam and the boys get on when they grew up?

Sam always showed favoritism to Jacob. He sent him to the most expensive college and David went to the community college and lived at home.

What did you do about this?

It was terrible. What could I do? Nothing! I could do nothing! You don't know what Sam was like. I saved money on the side, you know, out of my table money and gave it to David.

What year did Sam tell you he was going to leave?

1985.

The answer to this question showed the date of David's birth coincided with the time Sam was having his affair. These dates were the keys to Sam's treatment of his younger son. Ida began to suspect there was a relationship between the affair and David's birth. Sam had had five years to bond emotionally to Jacob, but he saw David as the reason he could not leave his marriage. We see that David was the recipient of Sam's anger, because Sam saw him as the reason he was "forced" to stay in the marriage. David was treated differently than his brother, and so he developed differently than his brother. This defined his personality.

The story doesn't end here, because family events have a ripple effect and repercussions are felt in all directions. Gradually, the follow-up to this affair led to other problems within the family. The first was in the relationship within the family-of-origin. The second appeared in the next generation.

"I guess this affected David. He and Jacob had an off-and-on-again relationship. They stuck together when there was a problem, but didn't have much contact as adults after they were married. I thought David was a good son despite Sam's unfair treatment of him when he was growing up. And what did he get for it? Nothing."

But more was going on in this family. A look at current stressors will complete this story.

Current Stressors

"David's wife, Judy, is having an affair. She fell in love with a man at work and she wants to leave the marriage. But, you know what, nobody ever knew about Sam's affair except for his brother and my sister. So it couldn't have affected David's marriage."

Ida was wrong about that. Although David did not know about his father's affair, he felt the tension and he was the child who carried the pain of the family. He couldn't understand his father's rejection of him. It never made sense to him because he felt he was a good child and nothing he did could change his father's treatment of him. Sam had emotionally abandoned David instead of guiding him through life. Sam was not differentiated enough to do this for David. This is a case of emotional cutoff without leaving the family.

As a result, David grew up needy and longing for intimacy, yet having no role model to learn from, and at times suffered from depression. He married a woman with personality traits like his father's, who was cold. His wife felt smothered by David's need for closeness. She, too, had problems with intimacy and paradoxically ran to another man's arms for comfort.

No one needed to know of the affair in order to react to the anxiety created by it in the family. Everyone was affected by it, including other generations. Had it stopped in the first generation, the story would have a happier ending. The way it would have stopped is for Sam and Ida to find the cause of his infidelity. A mink coat is nice, but it is not a cure.

Ida finally came to realize that David's source of anger at her developed because he did not see her as protecting him from his father's rejection. Ida acknowledged to David her husband's poor treatment of him and apologized for not protecting him. She plans to tell him that it resulted from his father's anger at her, but she is now struggling with how far she wants to go with the explanation.

How to Assess an Affair

It may seem that you cannot evaluate affairs of the heart. They are completely subjective and not given to such scrutiny. Some think it may take the glow off to look too closely, but others have found that it helps them make sense of the situation and most likely is better for them in the long run.

The following story provides an outline you can use to assess an affair. It will show you how to stand back and achieve some distance from the affair so that you can obtain more objectivity.

When you finish reading this example, you will find a similar guide in the Appendix, to fill out if you wish. The guide will bring together all the material you have read so far so that you can apply it to your situation. It will help you answer your question: Will he really leave her for me?

The Situation

Peg began her affair with a coworker, Lawrence. As you follow Peg's story, you will be able to see the way in which an affair can be looked at objectively.

"Lawrence and I both work for a large law firm and we met at a regional conference. It was my first conference and I was nervous. He sensed that and he really helped me throughout the conference. That was two years ago when I was forty and he was forty-six. I knew he was married, but that didn't matter because he was just helping a new employee.

"A month later he called me to go to dinner when he came to town, which he did frequently. Nothing happened the first time he came in for business, but we began to keep in touch by e-mail. He e-mailed me frequently and sometimes late at night. We started to IM each other and I began to share personal problems. I had quite a few. I had been widowed a year before and this was my first job after not ever working outside my home. My daughter was away at college, and I took a short course to learn to be a paralegal.

"I felt really close to him. He was a man I could share so much with. The next time he came in town, I invited him for dinner and we found ourselves becoming very physical with each other. He told me he was married, but at that point, I didn't care because he was so special. I figured I could share him and I would do nothing to interfere with his marriage, make no demands, no phone calls to his wife.

"In the spring of this year, I realized I wanted to marry him and also I became pregnant, which surprised me at my age. I didn't know what to do. What would I tell my daughter? What would people at work think? He was angry because I had been careless, and I saw a side of him I had never seen before. He wanted me to have an abortion, which I could not do. For two weeks it was terrible and I didn't know what to do. Nature solved the problem because I miscarried.

"Then he wanted to go on as before.

"We started to argue because he said he couldn't marry me even though he loved me. We have called it quits a few times and then we start back up again. I've felt very guilty through all of this. It's now Thanksgiving and he is no closer to a commitment and I am still lonely and confused."

Type of Affair

The first assessment that Peg needs to make is to identify the type of affair it is for her, and the type of affair it is for Lawrence.

For him: "It is a fling for him, but I mistook it for a romantic love affair."

For her: "It is a romantic love affair for me."

Current Stressors

The next issue that Peg needs to explore in assessment of the affair is what recent stressors might have led to the affair in the first place. Clearly, Peg was drawn to the affair because of the life transitions she was undergoing.

For her: "I was very lonely. My husband had died rather suddenly after contracting an unusual and overwhelming infection. We had a good marriage of twenty years and I missed him. We were high school sweethearts. My parents adored him. I wanted to do well at this conference and in my new job. I was frightened and Lawrence helped me. He was kind to me and I trusted him."

For him: "I don't know. He never talked much about anything except his work, and that was okay."

Family-of-Origin

For her: "I was brought up in a very traditional home in spite of the times. We kids were sent to private religious school. I know my mother's father had a series of affairs and it embarrassed Mom and made her very angry with him. My grandparents separated and Mom only saw her father at Christmas. That's when we saw him, too, and we all acted like nothing had ever happened. Her mother could not forgive him. My grandfather never remarried.

"My father was a family man, always looking out for our interests. My brother had an affair right before his tenth anniversary and my mother stopped talking to him until he remarried, and she is still a little cool to him."

For him: "Lawrence told me he was the oldest brother of three sisters and he had a lot of responsibility growing up, but that is all. I guess that is why he recognized my nervousness and helped. I think his father had an affair because he alluded to it after we watched a movie on video, but when I asked about it, he said it was nothing. So I don't know too much."

Preliminary Conclusions?

We are only partway done, but it is a place to stop and assess our preliminary understanding of Peg's affair. Then we can proceed to look at the other factors that enter into such an assessment.

For her: "I learned that because I feel a certain way, it doesn't mean he will feel the same way. I also learned that you have to be careful about these e-mails. It is like verbal foreplay. It just made me ready for that affair. The pregnancy brought everything to a head for me. It seemed like a gift, a chance to start again. I felt confused and than bewildered, and furthermore, here I was in a position of being the other woman. Although it's true, I somehow don't feel that's really me. I just couldn't believe what had happened in my life and to top it all off, Lawrence was not there for me. I realized that I was asking for something he never promised."

For him: "He only told me information about his work, nothing too personal. He was a really good listener. I was surprised at how angry he became when I got pregnant. I would not have thought that about him. It does matter that he is married, because it mattered a lot to him."

What Peg learned was important, but not important enough to save her from future heartbreak. There is more she needs to know.

A More Complete Understanding

Peg was coping with some difficult circumstances and in the beginning the affair was comforting to her. She was mourning the loss of her husband of twenty years. The loss of a spouse is a very stressful event at any time, but even more so when there is little or no forewarning and when it is premature. As sad as any death is for a spouse, a premature death is very difficult for the family. Peg, older than most women who start work today, had little confidence in her abilities. This, of course, did not mean she could not do the job; it only meant she was frightened. Another transition, but an expected one for Peg, was that her only child was away at college. This added to her cares when Lawrence, a mature man, came into her life.

Peg began to understand how transitions affect someone's life and the importance of dealing with them directly. Jumping into a relationship can cause you to repress your feelings, only to have them surface in the future. It can also cause you to look to others for help in meeting your needs.

We can also see that the generational history affects current issues. There was infidelity in both of their families. We know the reaction to infidelity resulted in an emotional cutoff. Her mother withdrew from her father and then her son because of their infidelity. This caused further stress to Peg. She worried what her mother and daughter would think of her. This put more pressure on her to pursue Lawrence when she felt his abandonment. Peg and Lawrence ended their affair. Peg began grieving for the many losses: her husband, her affair, her daughter's move from home, and her pregnancy. She did this in a group for young widows and widowers. She learned how to nurture herself and to develop new interests. She also learned more about loneliness and ways to cope.

> "It was a tough time for me. I didn't think I could go on without Lawrence, but I did. I had become so isolated. I had no one I could share this with until I met the women in my support group and began to feel comfortable. They were much more accepting of me than I was of myself."

In individual therapy, she began to explore her family's emotional system and she worked to end the emotional cutoff with her brother and her elderly grandfather.

When marital difficulties are not addressed, problems can result. One is that individuals may see an affair as a solution to their concerns. The resulting stress from ongoing unresolved issues might propel them into looking for someone with whom to spend some peaceful moments.

A more complete understanding of the past can help us cope with the present and avoid certain pitfalls in the future. Peg now has friends and more skills than she had earlier. She is better equipped emotionally for some of life's problems.

Putting It Together

You have now read much about affairs. You have looked at this information and how it applies to you. You may have said to yourself, "No way, that's not me," or, "Okay, that's right on target." Some information will fit like a glove, and some will not, because people are not all alike. Their motivations vary, their needs may be unique, and their circumstances different.

Now is the time to apply this information to your own circumstances. Hopefully, you will be able to stand back and view this with objectivity. As you've learned in the previous chapters, you first need to explore the story of your affair. Second, there are questions to ask yourself. You may come to a conclusion, or a tentative understanding of your experiences, or you may be processing the information. Processing means sorting through, thinking about what you have read, and relating it to your own life. If you were seeing a therapist, you would be discussing the situation in this way. Essentially, what you are doing through this process is reorganizing the information so that you have a way to process it.

Peg's story was an example of how it is done. Not all affairs are alike nor are people's circumstances. The questions some individuals will need to consider may not be valid for other people. With this in mind, you will find a Form for Assessing Your Affair similar to Peg's in the Appendix, but including questions to consider that will cover many individual differences. It is designed to help you assess your affair and I strongly urge you to use it. I suggest you fill out the form, put it aside, and then reread it a few weeks later. This will give you time to process your thinking.

Finding the Answer to His Intentions

Once you have an objective picture of your affair, you have two choices: one, to end the affair; and two, to try to change it. If you find you cannot change it, you have eliminated that as an option and you are left with the decision to stay or to go. If you stay and you are not able to make changes, then you are still in a powerless situation. Hoping that it will change is not a realistic option. In trying to change it, the first step is to recognize your rights and to ask for them. This requires speaking assertively, openly, and honestly—not aggressively.

If the affair has reached a point where you want to discuss the future and you feel the romance is at a standstill, then you can ask him about his intentions. This means that you can speak *assertively* in requesting clarification of the situation. When you do, you must know that the consequences of addressing this issue may be that the affair will end.

Speaking Assertively

Even with all the gains women have made in the years since the Women's Revolution, some women find they can speak up in the boardroom, but not the bedroom. It is your right to express your needs openly and honestly, but with respect for the person to whom you are speaking. In affairs this step is often ignored and couples go directly to yelling at each other when the difficult subject comes up of where the relationship is going. When you approach the discussion, there are certain guidelines to follow that will lead to a more productive dialogue.

General Guidelines

- Schedule your talk when there is enough time for discussion.
- Use an "I" statement to say how you feel and what you would like to happen.
- If you find you did not phrase your thoughts well, or you have something to add to what you already said, you can say what you want later, the next day, or another time. Remember to express yourself in an assertive manner.
- Assertive communication can promote intimacy and can lead to problem-solving.

Understanding Communication Styles

There are four styles of communication to recognize:

Aggressive: raised voice, exaggerated hand gestures, demanding, angry, obviously coercive, frightening to the other person

Passive: quiet, do what you are told, head bowed, do not express needs, "doormat," obviously noncoercive

Passive-aggressive: quiet, do not express needs, do not show anger, speaker has a "gotcha" attitude, covertly coercive

Assertive: honest and open communication with respect for everyone's rights, nonthreatening, obviously noncoercive

How It Works

The first examples will show how assertive communication works. After that is understood, you will be able to apply what you have learned to the issue of his intentions.

Jennifer is angry that Clark has called again at the last minute to cancel their dinner tonight. Something has come up regarding his daughter's wedding plans, but he says he and Jennifer will get together tomorrow night. Here are some possible scenarios.

Aggressive: "I can't believe this. Not again. I see where I stand with you. I always come second. I'm sick of this. Just don't call until you're ready to treat me better. I don't want to see you tomorrow night." She hangs up and cries.

Results: They are both angry and feel misunderstood. No communication results from this, just resentment.

Passive: "Okay, I'll see you tomorrow night."

Results: She is hurt and feels he can do what he wants with immunity.

Passive-aggressive: "Okay, I'll see you tomorrow night." But she plans to call him the last minute and cancel, just as he has done to her.

Results: He will feel confused when she cancels because she said it was okay. She will feel that she showed him, but nothing is cleared up and it will happen again. She has the "gotcha" attitude.

Assertive: "I can understand how this can happen, Clark, but I am disappointed because it has been happening a lot. I feel used when I am treated this way. I will see you tomorrow night, but I want to discuss this and see what can be done about it."

Results: Each person feels understood. It doesn't change the situation for that evening, but it opens up discussion and probably will lead to some type of compromise. The discussion may help you know where this relationship is ultimately going.

In the "aggressive" example, Clark would probably have answered in anger and become defensive. In the passive, he would have no clue as to how Jennifer was feeling or that there was a problem. In the passive and passive-aggressive, he would have felt badly or wondered about her reaction and been angry, just as Jennifer was after being treated the same way. More importantly Clark would not understand what Jennifer was feeling. In the assertive response, he would have listened and more than likely answered without anger. This would result in a discussion about his treatment of her, which would give Jennifer the opportunity to explain how she sees it and might lead to problem-solving.

Two important thoughts to keep in mind when speaking assertively:

If you miss the opportunity to say what's on your mind, you can always be assertive later. In this situation, Jennifer did not respond the way she wanted, and she called the next day:

> "Clark, when you called and canceled last night, I was hurt because you do it so often that I feel unimportant and taken for granted. I can understand it happening now and then, but not as frequently as it does. I would prefer you make arrangements to get together when the chances are excellent that we can. Then I can make other plans and not sit around with nothing to do and feeling bad."

The answer Jennifer may get:

> "I appreciate how you feel. I'm sorry. It was thoughtless. I'll be more considerate."

A second important factor is not to be assertive if it will put you in any kind of danger. If you are in a relationship in which you are physically, sexually, or emotionally abused, you risk being hurt by being assertive. Instead, you should see a therapist to help you understand why you are in such a relationship. This will enable you to sort through why you want to be with him, and if you decide to leave, you will have the support to do so safely.

Applying This to the Big Picture

Jennifer started being assertive on the smaller issues of fairness in how Clark treats her. But if she wants to know more about their future, she could practice her communication skills on smaller issues and then proceed to her big question: Will he really leave her to marry me?

Jennifer could also practice using her assertive communication with little risk by trying *mental rehearsal,* a technique described by Dr. Maxwell Maltz in his book *Psycho-Cybernetics.* Imagine yourself in any situation that is new or that you feel might cause you discomfort or anxiety. You can do this to practice or rehearse your communication skills. Mentally review what you want to say and have the conversation with your lover in your mind. Test your responses until you are comfortable with that scenario. Your mental rehearsal will give you the opportunity to correct mistakes or change the events to your satisfaction. In the real situation, you may not get the answer you want, but by doing the mental rehearsal repeatedly, you will feel more comfortable in the actual situation. It is beneficial to practice your mental rehearsal while relaxed. In Chapter 10, there is a description of progressive muscle relaxation that you might want to refer to. This rehearsal will desensitize you to the anxiety of the situation. Rehearsing it is as good as doing it. You are now prepared. You have done much to work through your anticipatory anxiety about an honest discussion with your lover.

To truly assess where you are in this relationship, you need to know his intentions or plans for your future together. You must be prepared for an answer you do not want to hear. You also need to be aware of whether or not he is being truthful. Once you've determined his true intentions, you need to examine what that means for you and your future:

- If you are told that the relationship will remain as it is, that is, an affair, then you need to decide if you are willing to be second to his family. This will go back to what your goals are for yourself. Then, if you continue the affair, it is with the full knowledge that he will not leave her for you. You have the choice of continuing or leaving.

- If he tells you that maybe it will be different in a month, a year, or more, and he asks that you give him more time, you need to be realistic. Will he really change his mind after you have spent more time together? If you believe that to be true, then try to imagine him giving you the same negative answer four years from now. Think of how you will feel continuing as you are with no promise of marriage. If you want to have children, consider your age and the reality of the situation. Are you willing to sacrifice your life's goals for the possibility of another rejection?

- If he tells you that he will not leave his wife, it will leave you with a sense of loss, depression, and anger. You may feel that you have sacrificed so much for the relationship that you are too exhausted to start anew. It may seem overwhelming to start over, but you need to decide if you are really willing to spend years in a relationship that is headed nowhere. This is a wake-up call to rebuild your life.

- If he says he will leave her and marry you, you must evaluate the situation carefully to be sure he is being honest and look for behavior that supports that answer. Most importantly, you must also monitor your own feelings to be sure this is really what you want.

You need to be on guard for the stall, the lie, and for another date to come and go. You can get more specific by using your new communication skills. If the affair does not end abruptly after a serious discussion of the future, typically the affair continues with a certain amount of breaking up and coming together. This will lead you down a course of considering whether the affair is in your best interests. Speaking assertively will give you an idea of his intensions.

> *Donna:* Jim, I've waited for your three kids to graduate. Now you are asking me to wait for six more months, until after Christmas. Tell me what exactly will happen after Christmas.
>
> *Jim:* I don't know. I'm feeling pressure here, Donna, and I don't like it.

This is the point where a discussion can deteriorate into an argument and you will end up angry and with an inconclusive answer.

> *Donna:* I am sorry that you feel pressured, but since I have waited for four years, I am asking what will happen specifically after Christmas.
>
> *Jim:* For Pete's sake, Donna. I don't know.
>
> *Donna:* Okay, then think about it and give me an answer. Right after Christmas, we'll talk about it.

No big decisions were made during this conversation, but movement was happening in the relationship. Donna did not give Jim an ultimatum, bring up the past, or berate him. She simply presented the evidence and then said they would think about it and talk again. They concluded the conversation without saying things they would regret. They both have time now to process what was said and to think about it over the next six months. Now Donna needs to review her options and not bring this up again until the agreed-upon period is over. She is not remaining powerless. By speaking assertively, she is regaining her power in the relationship.

If you feel, after reading the guidelines for assertive communication, that your way of expressing yourself needs improvement, remember to start on a smaller goal rather than a large one. For example, it would be better to start with your feelings on being at his beck and call rather than your need to know if he is going to leave his wife. Learn to express yourself assertively, and practice. These are skills that will always be helpful to you in other situations as well. Then you can move toward the discussion of your future. If the results of your discussion are that you, he, or both of you decide to end the affair, you will need to heal from this experience.

The possibilities are to continue as you are, to end the affair, or to marry. If you were seeing a therapist to talk over your feelings, at this point, you would look at the choices available to you and the consequences of them. In the next section, we will do just that.

Part IV

Coping with the Decisions

Chapter Eight

Continuing with the Affair

*W*hen an affair goes on for a long time without reaching a resolution, it will develop into an arrangement in which the man will continue in his marriage and still maintain the affair. This may be due to many factors, one of which is ambivalence. The affair can continue for the duration of his marriage or the remainder of his life.

A Fictional Long-Term Affair

As mentioned earlier, the movie *The Pilot's Wife*, based on the novel of the same name by Anita Shreve, depicts an excellent example of a long-term affair, and explaining its plot gives us an intimate look at the information discussed so far.

When the film opens, it is night in a small oceanfront town in New England, and there is a knock at the door of the home of Kathryn Lyons. Her life is about to turn upside down. An investigator from the airline's union breaks the news that a 747 has crashed off the coast of Ireland. Kathryn's husband, Jack, is the pilot. Soon her home is occupied by other investigators. It becomes clear from the questions that they are concerned about the pilot and his activities prior to leaving home. The crash was the result of an explosion they say, but the cause remains unclear. Kathryn is puzzled by the turn the investigation is taking.

But life goes on and Kathryn finds a piece of paper with a phone number on it while looking through Jack's clothing as she does the laundry. In the midst of all of this tension, the Lyons's thirteen-year-old daughter, Mattie, astounds her mother by telling her that she has had sex so that she could stop thinking about it and just get it out of the way. Mattie asks her mother if it surprises her. After Kathryn tells her she is surprised, the daughter says, "See, you can't really know anyone." This prepares us for what will soon be revealed.

Kathryn starts her own investigation by dialing the phone number she found in Jack's clothing. This leads her to a small home in Ireland where a young, attractive woman named Muire Boland answers the door. Soon Kathryn meets Muire's infant son and young daughter. It is not long before Kathryn understands that Jack is the children's father and that he has been having a long-term love affair. Surprisingly, Muire knows about Kathryn and her daughter, Mattie.

Muire excuses herself to answer the telephone. Kathryn can tell by the quiet voice and the length of the conversation that important plans are being made. While waiting, Kathryn opens drawers and closets. She sees an established home with pictures of a family. During this time, Muire's daughter tells Kathryn her grandmother in America gave her the doll she is playing with.

Kathryn sees a photograph of Jack and Muire and learns from Muire that they were married in a Catholic church four years ago. Muire tells her Jack attended church regularly and that her daughter's doll is a gift from Jack's mother. When Kathryn objects and says that Jack never attends church and his mother is dead, Muire says that Jack's mother lives in a nursing home in the United States.

The audience is left to wonder: Who is the pilot's wife?

In flashbacks we learn that Kathryn had visited a priest to discuss burial without a body. She tells him that she and Jack were very happily married and that the early stages of their marriage had one kind of happiness and the later stages another. This tells us that the passion has leveled off or declined in their marriage, but she believes they have reached another level of contentment. Yet, in another flashback, we see her angrily entering Jack's office, where he is on the computer late at night, and telling him that he spends more time on the computer than he does with her. His response is angry and he forcefully throws the computer from the second-floor balcony to the floor below, smashing it to pieces. It may have been that Kathryn walked in on an e-mail communication Jack was having with Muire. The viewers begin to realize that there are problems either with Jack or with the marriage.

It seems that not only has the passion diminished in their marriage but so has their emotional intimacy. Jack hid his mother's existence and the importance of the church in his life from Kathryn. There is also the hint that he is staying in the marriage only because of his daughter, Mattie. From what we see, Jack's commitment to his marriage is questionable at best. Jack is a man who at midlife, dissatisfied with his life, made the choice to have a long-term affair.

Kathryn, on the other hand, had been in denial about the state of her marriage and ignored obvious clues. She was devastated by the discovery of her husband's second family in Ireland. She *obsessively reviewed* the facts until she could understand them. In the final scene, back in the United States, Kathryn and Mattie walk up the steps to the nursing home to introduce themselves to Jack's mother.

At one point in the movie, the viewer learns that Jack carried money back and forth for financing political activities in Ireland. On his final flight, his bag was switched with one that had a bomb. The Irish wife is eventually arrested for her terrorist activities. The picture ends without mention of what was to become of his Irish children, and if Jack had made any provisions for their support in the event of his death.

Such a fictional account of a long-term affair leads to other questions that apply to real-life long-term affairs. A long-term affair is like dynamite, ready to explode at any moment. In this case, it was Jack's premature death. Where would the story have taken us if Jack had reached retirement age? Would he have retired in the United States or Ireland? How much did the economic factors enter into it? It takes a wealthy man to support two families in his retirement. What would have happened if Jack had died a natural death, leaving two wives and the children he had with each of them? If Kathryn in her old age discovered the affair, would she have felt her entire life had been a sham, a mockery? Did Jack ever intend to tell his children of his two marriages, or did he hope that somehow it would all end without one knowing about the other? Jack did more than cheat on his American wife—he cheated all his children of the exclusivity and loyalty that they deserved.

Although *The Pilot's Wife* is a fictional account of a long-term affair, author Anita Shreve is right on target. Anyone woman entering into a long-term affair needs to consider the possible ramifications. An affair affects more than just the two people involved.

The Choices

When an affair continues for a significant length of time, it is often because it has developed into a romantic love affair and the couple for some reason has not married. When an affair has reached the romantic love-affair stage, there are a few ways it can play out and choices the couple can make.

Drifting

The couple can go on as they are, just drifting along. The problem with this is that a decision has not been made. Therefore, the couples who are drifting along have not reached stage four of the affair, where they have agreed upon an answer. They are stuck in stage three: disequilibrium. This means they are back to the seesaw of breakup and reconciliations, or pursuing and distancing. Everything can go smoothly until she decides she really wants an answer about their future. So they start their dance and then return to the status quo. This can be a long-term affair without direction. One member of a support group started talking about her "boyfriend," and this is what she told the group.

> *Ruthie:* "He said we were happy and he was good to me, so we should let it go at that and just continue. In a way he is right. I wasn't happy before and I had nothing to look forward to. But I did reach a point about a year ago when I was arguing about what was going to happen with us, and that was a bad time. So now I just go with the flow and most of the time I think maybe it will change and I put the whole thing out of my mind. I mean, I try to."

If the affair just drifts along while she continues to hope, as Ruthie is doing, the chances diminish that he will leave his wife to marry her. Most importantly, if you are in this type of situation, you lose control over your own destiny. You are still waiting for him to make the decisions about your life. You are not empowered.

A long-term affair just drifting along was revealed in the Dear Abby column (May 22, 2005) in newspapers across the country. A woman identifying herself as "Can't Stop Crying in Texas," wrote to say she had been the "other woman" for thirty years, even though she knew her lover had cheated on her for ten of those years, just as he cheated on his wife. After his wife died a year ago, he told "Crying" that he could no longer spend every night at her house because of his grandchildren. "Crying" discovered that he has been involved with another woman for the past three months. He told the other woman he could only see her a few nights a week because he sees a special friend—"Crying"! Most other couples don't drift this long without coming to some understanding about their expectations of each other. "Crying" said, "He didn't respect me enough to be honest from the start."

An Agreement

Others involved in a long-term affair talk about their future. They usually agree to go on as they are, knowing there will be no marriage for one reason or another. They most likely have reached the romantic love-affair stage, but will not marry.

> *Luanne:* "He loves me and I know it. I know he would marry me if he could. Staying was my choice. I am doing this with my eyes open."

There are several possible reasons he may choose to stay with his wife: his children, his religion, his job, health concerns, his marriage, or financial considerations.

England's Prince Charles and Camilla Parker Bowles fall into this category. After his marriage to Princess Diana, the desire to be with his old flame overpowered Charles's marriage vows and he and Camilla continued their affair. The odds of a divorce for Charles seemed impossible at that time because he was heir to the throne. It was almost seven and a half years after Diana's death that Prince Charles and Camilla Parker Bowles announced they would marry.

Coexisting

There are long-term marriages in which the wife knows about her husband's lover and will coexist with the situation as it is. He may have told her about you and she is aware of the role you play in her life. She most likely has made it clear what she will and won't tolerate about having you in her life. This usually includes an agreement to conduct the affair discreetly and to keep it from children and other family members, as well as certain commitments concerning family vacations, family events, and how the family money is spent. She will know that there are certain times he will not be available because he is with you, his lover. They have worked out an arrangement in which the wife allows the affair to continue. In this case, like the previous one, you will know the answer to your question. He will not leave her to marry you. And he may leave you at some point in the future.

A Parallel "Marriage"

There are other couples whose long-term affair is actually a "parallel marriage" for the man. This relationship may differ in intensity from the "coexisting" long-term affair because there may be children from this liaison and because the man is as deeply involved as though he were married to the lover. For example, he will go on vacations with her and attend public events. There are women who are happy with this arrangement. She may have children with him and if she cannot marry him, she feels that she is tied to him through the children and that the chance that he will be in her life improves because of this.

As for the man, he may want this because he loves her and this is a way to be with her when he cannot marry her. But it is not always love that keeps him in the long-term affair. Some men find that being in a triangle keeps them from having to make a real commitment to either their marriage or their lover. This way they do not have to be emotionally close to either person. Other men feel more powerful and have more control when they can have two families and, of course, that means two queens. It really is good to be the king!

Charles Lindbergh, the American hero and the first pilot to make a solo nonstop transatlantic crossing, had a second family in Germany. Like the fictional Jack Lyons of *The Pilot's Wife*, Lindbergh had freedom and an excuse to cross the Atlantic frequently. It was easy for him to have another family privately and away from the public eye. In 1957 at the age of fifty-five, Lindbergh met a young Munich woman named Brigitte Hesshaimer. They had three children, Dyrk, Astrid, and Lester, who were born between 1958 and 1967. Lindbergh's wife, Anne

Morrow Lindbergh, was in her early fifties when her husband fathered his second family. Anne and Charles Lindbergh had six children together.

The *Guardian* newspaper (28 August 2003) reported that DNA samples from Lindbergh's American family and the three children of his German family were compared, proving that Lindbergh was the father of the three children with Brigitte Hesshaimer. *Father unknown* is on their birth certificate; Lindbergh's name is not. His German children found 150 love letters to their mother from Lindbergh signed "C."—for his assumed name of Careu Kent. He supported them financially until his death and helped them buy a small house. Two years after Lindbergh's death, his German children approached his American family with the letters and photographs. At first they were met "with frosty silence," but the children of the two families have met and are trying to establish their relationship.

The famous architect of the twentieth century, Louis Kahn, had children resulting from two long-term affairs. He fathered a daughter, Alex, with Anne Tying, an architect in his office. Later, after that affair ended, he had a son, Nathaniel, with Harriet Pattison, a landscape artist. He also had a daughter, Sue Ann, from his marriage to his wife, Esther. Both Anne Tying and Harriet Pattison had wanted him to marry them and were hurt by his refusal. In talking about her situation, Nathaniel's mother said, "It was humiliating," that is, the inability to be acknowledged—to be hidden, and not to be able to be seen with Kahn publicly. Then she added, "It was worth it." All the women lived within several miles of each other, but their paths never crossed. The story of the parallel lives of Louis Kahn became known from the film *My Architect*, produced by his son Nathaniel in an attempt to know more about the father he so longed for. The film is a son's "quest to understand Kahn both as architect and father."

Louis Kahn died at the age of seventy-three when his son was eleven. Nathaniel remembers that his father visited their home about once a week, but there was no physical evidence that he had ever been there. Harriet Pattison's brothers hated Kahn for what had happened and her sister described Harriett as "lacking in realism." As for Nathaniel, his secret wish was that his father would come and live at his home. That never materialized, nor did his wishes for more frequent visits from his father. All the women were bitter. Esther sent messages that no one should come to the funeral, but Nathaniel and his mother did.

In the film, all Louis Kahn's children met and talked over their lives. They wondered if in some strange way they were a family. This happened also with Lindbergh's two families. When children try to relate to the children a parent had with another person, it is difficult for them to reconcile and integrate it into their knowledge of their own history. Charles Kuralt, the *On the Road* reporter for CBS, had a secret second "marriage" for twenty-nine years with Patricia Elizabeth Shannon, whom he met when he had already been married for six years. She knew Kuralt was married, but they maintained their secret easily because she lived in a rural area of Montana. Shannon said that Kuralt supported her well. He spent about "$600,000 during the first decade" and "$400,000 to help her start a small business." He also paid for the education of two of her three children, a $50,000 cottage in Ireland, and land in Montana.

Shannon believed that Kuralt would get a divorce at some point. She said in her deposition, "I went through bouts of despair and there were arguments, but we never directly talked about his life in New York. I knew it existed. . . . I did not inquire into it and he didn't discuss it with me."

These real-life stories clearly show that there are serious consequences of a long-term affair. You need to weigh them carefully.

The Consequences

An affair is very serious business, but when it is long-term, it can be dangerous. It can be catastrophic to all involved because it exists simultaneously with the marriage. Its effects go on for generations for all the children. You lose out in many ways as well. You make sacrifices and often don't fulfill important goals for yourself, because you spend your life living in the shadows. Before entering into such an arrangement, think carefully of all the consequences.

If You Have Children

One definite consequence of affairs is that someone always gets hurt, and it is not just those making up the triangle. When children are involved, the consequences can be even more painful. This is true of the children whose parents are having the affair, as well as children born from the relationship. Children resulting from a long-term affair are confused about the situation no matter how well they are loved and cared for. They either have no father with whom to identify and to help them navigate the myriad experiences they will face as they grow up, or they have a father whom they see irregularly. Some are suspicious about their situation, but others may not be aware of it. When they find out, they may have a strong reaction. Many children are aware that their friends' parents are divorced, but they still have a father. Some may know a friend whose father is dead. But children from a long-term affair know *their* situation is unique, and they all long for that father and for a normal family experience.

Finding out that their father has another family is challenging even for older children who are mature and worldly.

Amir, the narrator in the bestselling novel *The Kite Runner*, describes the devastating effect that can come from infidelity that produces children even when they are not aware of the situation. Amir discovers in adulthood that his best friend, Hassan, was the result of an affair his father, Baba, had with Hassan's mother. Hassan's family lived in Baba's complex and were his servants. The children played as brothers would. Baba was very kind and loving to Hassan, causing Amir to be exceptionally jealous of Hassan and confused by his father's devotion to him. As a result of these feelings, Amir failed to save Hassan from a situation, with disastrous consequences that lasted their entire lifetime.

Another example is that of, Janet, a thirty-five-year-old mother of twin girls, who became a client after the death of her mother. She was so devastated over her mother's death four months earlier that she spent excessive time in bed. She could no longer function. Her doctor referred her for counseling because he could find no physical cause for her behavior. After a short time, Janet then revealed her pain was not just due to the death of her mother, but was more complex.

Janet: "My mother called me in to tell me something shortly before she died. It was a secret she held for years. It seems that the man I love and call my father is not really my father. Mr. X, our next-door neighbor while I was growing up, is my biological father. He and my mother had an affair for years. They wanted to marry, but Mrs. X would not give him a divorce and so all the grownups knew, but my brother and the next-door kids didn't. My best friend is Mandy X, and now I find out we are stepsisters or something. I am sick. I don't know if she knows. What am I suppose to do? I can't even express how I feel. I'm angry with my mother and it seems we just buried her. I keep going over and over our lives and what this means."

Children, regardless of their age, feel a sense of confusion and betrayal of the family when they discover a parent's affair. The identity and issues of family loyalty can become problematic for children of all ages. Lester, a man of thirty-eight, says of his father:

"He wants me to meet his #%$X#Z mistress! I know what is going on and I don't like it. My mother was there for him all her life. He used to be proud of my mother, but now he is ashamed."

Lester's father, John, is a lawyer whose wife, Carol, became mentally ill in her sixties. His father, having worked hard all of his life, looked forward to a wonderful retirement in Florida where he felt the weather was conducive to the lifestyle he wanted. He decided to find the happiness he had worked so hard for. He took classes, went to concerts, and swam and ran every day. One day, he started talking to a woman, Jessica, at the pool and found that they had a lot in common. She was a widow and she, too, was active in classes and community projects. In particular, she was active in legal services for the poor and soon convinced John to volunteer for her cause.

Jessica was attractive and well known in her community for her philanthropic activities. She knew John was married and about the problems that he faced with his wife. They agreed to this arrangement because John would not divorce Carol. Even though Jessica understood and accepted that decision, Jessica wanted him to leave Carol and marry her. They essentially agreed to a long-term affair.

John joined his son Lester in a counseling session.

Lester: Dad, can you understand this is my mother?

John: Yes, of course. Can you understand this is my life? Lester, you are too young to understand a person's desire for happiness when the days left are so much fewer than in the past. I have always been a devoted and good husband and would never have spent time with another woman if Carol even remotely resembled the woman I married.

They came to see each other's point of view. Even though the prescribed medications brought some symptoms under control, Carol was no longer the same woman or companion for John. Instead of being home alone, Carol was registered in an adult day care center for the mentally ill and John agreed to go to a weekly support group for the family members. John maintained his affair with Jessica. He agreed not to badger his son about meeting Jessica, but continued to hope that Lester would relent and allow Jessica to be part of his world. Lester came to accept his father's solution, but could never condone it.

This family believed that this was the best solution they could reach in an imperfect world.

A Life of Exclusion

If you choose to continue the affair with the understanding that it will remain as it is, you must recognize that your life of exclusion will continue as such. You may now feel freer to share your romance with friends because you feel that it has taken on a type of permanency, but you will not be able to be part of his children's lives, his work, or his social life.

It also means missing the important celebrations of the rites of passage. When he is enjoying his children's accomplishments, you will be once again sitting on the sidelines. If he receives any honors or awards, you will not be there to see it. Your celebration will be private. Conversely, it means the same for you. He will most likely not be by your side for the rites of passage or significant occasions in your life. In reality, you are going it alone.

You will not be by his side if he is ill, and it may be hard to reach him at such a time. You will not be privy to health reports. It is his family who will be there.

One final heart-wrenching rite of passage is his death, and you will be alone and mourn alone.

Another Family

If you become involved in a long-term affair and decide to have a family together, it is important that you consider the consequences of that decision. If you believe that having children will keep him by your side, married or not, you may be mistaken about the quality of the relationship.

Elsa, the first woman I ever saw in this situation, is etched in my mind because of the sadness and despair I saw as she sat in my office with a sleeping baby in a stroller. Her lover agreed to support the child, and that was the extent of what he would do.

She was shocked at his callousness because she remembered the passion in their meetings and she mistook it for love. They had been together for two years when he became engaged to someone else! Although she knew about it, she said she loved him so much that she couldn't stop seeing him. Then she found out she was pregnant, but by then he was actively planning his wedding. He was married before the child was born.

> *Elsa:* "I have only my sister to help me and every day she calls me stupid. I feel so alone, but I love my little boy."

My client felt abandoned, which indeed she was.

I have also worked with couples in which a child was born from a long-term affair. The mother adores and loves her child. The wife typically wants her husband to have very limited contact with the child. The husband is usually torn between his child and his other family.

Working out the details of how visitations are handled, the role of the child's mother, and trying to keep the best interests of the child in mind can become very complex. The emotional well-being of all the parties must be considered. The father wants a relationship with his child, his wife wants boundaries so the affair does not resume, and both are concerned about how the child will be integrated into their family life. The wife has a proprietary interest in her children, and the lover wants her child or children recognized and treated well.

Sometimes that happens, other times it does not. It all depends on the maturity of the people involved and whether they will put emotions aside to think through the situation to come to the best solution for everyone involved.

His Death

Your lover can die at any point in the affair and at any age. In marriages, there is some preparation for this event; in affairs there may be little or no discussion of this. In a marriage, there is usually talk of one's wishes, both financial and emotional. The wife will hear the following phrases, which the lover may not hear:

> *If anything happens, I want the children to . . .*
> *Don't cash in the government bonds . . .*
> *Take care of my mother, and visit her at Christmas.*
> *Don't resuscitate if . . .*
> *I want to be buried, cremated . . .*

It's considered part of the advanced planning of married couples. These are bleak discussions to have, but they belong in the realm of marriage. It is just one more example of how you will be left out, even at the end of his life. That is the reality of the long-term affair. The wife will have a support system of family and friends. She will be able to grieve openly and she will have the ritual of a funeral or a memorial service to help her through the dark days. You will probably not have that. It is hard to keep a long-term affair a secret, so some may know and you will receive a degree of comfort from them. It will be more difficult for you if you are a married woman who is grieving for a lover of many years. If your husband does not know about your lover, he will not understand your depression, and if he knows, your grief will be a source of his despair and anger. You will not be as free as the wife to express yourself emotionally.

Maggie's story shows just how devastating this situation can be. She sat in my office, crying and telling me about the emptiness in her life. This is a summary of what had transpired and how she was feeling.

"About two years ago, Walt died. We have had a relationship that lasted eight years. That's longer than some marriages. I thought I could handle it, but I am still grieving. I knew after the first two years that we would not be getting married. I wanted him to and we quarreled about it, but finally I realized that it wasn't going to happen. But I felt that we had such a special bond that we could remain as we were.

"It was really terrible. When I found out he died, I was driving on the Beltway listening to the news. He was a well-known figure and he had been in an auto accident. I had to drive onto the shoulder to pull myself together. I was shocked.

"I went to the funeral. His family didn't know me and I knew there would be many people there in this very large church. I felt very left out. In a way I was lucky I could even attend. I went home feeling depleted and I haven't recovered.

"I had made a deal in my heart, 'Till death do us part.'"

The wife will also have a will and a financial plan. If you are a married woman having this affair, you may not have the financial concerns that some single women might. For single women, having their own careers and plans for retirement, this may not be an issue. For others, there may be financial considerations that were never discussed.

If you and your lover have children, financial considerations are very important. He is responsible for helping you with the food, clothing, shelter, and hopefully the extras like piano lessons and college expenses.

Thinking It Through

If you know he will not give her up to marry you and you have discussed a long-term affair with him, there are very important questions you must ask yourself before you make such an agreement. Because it is often hard to look into the future and try to ascertain our feelings, I advise thinking about one question each night until you have completed the list. Try to imagine the consequences and how you might really feel about the situation each question suggests to you.

1. Are you willing to stay in this relationship with the knowledge that he will never marry you?
2. Are you willing to give up marriage to someone else whom you probably will never meet because you are committed to this arrangement?

3. If you are single without children, are you willing to give up becoming a mother?

4. If you and he should have children, will you be satisfied with raising them alone?

5. If the child is born with a severe lifelong health problem, will you feel you can raise and care for him alone day after day without support from his father?

6. If your child is seriously hurt or becomes ill, can you care for her alone while the father is alive and living with his other family?

7. Will you (and your child) be satisfied when his father cannot attend your child's school events, athletic activities, or ballet recital?

8. If you and he should have children, will you be satisfied with having them be the result of an affair?

9. Will you be comfortable explaining your child's paternity?

10. If you commit to this relationship on his terms, are you willing to continue living a life in secrecy?

11. Are you willing to give up personal goals if this relationship calls for it?

12. Are you willing to give up career goals if this relationship calls for it?

13. Can you accept all the limitations that will be imposed upon you by this relationship?

14. Can you trust him to be faithful to you?

15. Can you depend on him to assume any financial obligation that this relationship requires?

16. Will you be content if he ends this agreement sometime down the line?

17. Will you be content if for any reason he moves out of the area?

18. Will you be content if at some point down the road he ends the affair for his own reasons and you never see him again?

19. Will this relationship last if he has a sudden change in his health, his economic or career status, or that of his family?

20. When you are elderly, will you be content looking back on your life?

21. If he is much older, will you feel you made the right choice when he becomes ill or when he dies?

If your answer is not "yes" to every question, you may be giving up more than you realize to be with this man. I suggest you think carefully about your losses and find someone to marry who will give you a better chance at happiness. Jimmy the Greek, the once-famous oddsmaker, probably would have said, if you enter a long-term affair with a married man who will not leave her for you, "The deck is stacked against you on this one."

I'm with Jimmy on that.

Chapter Nine

You and He Marry

*Y*our question has been answered—he is going to leave her and marry you. If he has done this in a responsible manner by having individual and couples counseling, as discussed earlier, then the adjustment to this transition, although difficult, may be somewhat eased. It may have been helpful to his wife, but she will undoubtedly feel devastated about this major event in her life.

You will now emerge from the shadows, and you will have to deal with reality.

Coping with the Aftermath

You can expect that his extended family along with his immediate family will have strong reactions to his leaving his wife and marrying you. It is part of your responsibility as a couple to recognize this and conduct your lives and relate to them in a manner that is conducive to helping them heal. The purpose of this chapter is to help you understand his wife and children and to offer suggestions to make this transition as smooth as possible. This chapter will present some guidelines to help you as well, so you can ease into this transition with as little difficulty as possible. If you had premarital counseling, you will be more aware of the reality of day-to-day living together and how it differs from the secrecy of an affair. This chapter will present strategies to cope with your adjustment of living together. An important aspect of this is awareness of the others affected by your affair.

We will start with where the pain is: his family.

Empathy for His Former Wife

You and he will be very caught up with plans for your future together and the immediate tasks of introducing him to your family, friends, and colleagues who make up your world. They may not have met him yet, or, for that manner, may not even know about him. You will be experiencing the joy that comes from planning the wedding, and finding and decorating your new home together. But amidst all the joy, there are wounded people, so there is work for you and your new husband to do. It is your responsibility to recognize their wounds and the havoc that has been created in the lives of people who loved him and who probably felt that he would always be there for them. They are experiencing the end of what they envisioned their future to be.

His wife, in particular, is experiencing the death of her marriage. This, for her, is an unexpected transition. She will experience disbelief and an acute sense of betrayal until she can accept this major change in her life. She will go through the stages of grieving as in a death. In view of this, how would you expect her to behave toward you? How does she see her life now? From her perspective, she sees destruction all around her. She can see no future because she is still recovering. She may lose friends, status, and self-esteem, as well as her dreams. She sees a lonely life, and she feels you are in a large part to blame. You must realize the enormous pain she is experiencing as a result of your romance with her husband, the dissolution of her marriage, and your union with him. Even though she may hate and loathe you, you must stand back and try to understand what it must feel like to be in her place. Put yourself in her shoes by imagining the same thing happening to you five years down the road. Being able to do this is empathy. It is not pity or sympathy, but trying to understand her emotional world. This is important to do, even if you feel she is to blame because she didn't understand him and she nagged him. You must recognize that this may not be true. Even if it were, it will not help your marriage if you hold on to these feelings.

Until you recognize this, I do not believe it will be a comfortable journey for you. If you can see the situation from her viewpoint, you will grow and be better equipped to handle what the future might hold. If, instead of understanding, you become angry, adversarial, and lash back, you will not be on solid ground. It will only add stress and tension to your marriage. She may be confrontational because she is desperate about what is happening to her life. You might feel the same way if it were the reverse. If you can get past her anger and feel her despair, you may be more apt to come to decisions on future issues that will undoubtedly arise, and be able to get past your differences.

You can expect her to be very emotionally reactive immediately after discovery and for some time after that. It may take two years or more for her to heal and start to build a new life, but gradually, the tension will ease.

Blending the Families

If there are children, you will need to understand that they will be affected now and for years to come. You must try to coexist with her in as civil a way as possible. The best interests of the children need to be in your thoughts as you make this important decision. Psychiatrist Alfred Adler noted that children observe very well, but often interpret inaccurately. It is very important to be aware of their reactions, so that you can clear up any misinterpretations they may have made.

His Children

She is the mother of his children. You must keep from getting in the middle over issues with the children. In theory it is easy; in reality it is difficult, but it is important that you not become part of a triangle. This would make the children pawns in the adult interactions.

Young Children

When boundaries are clear, everyone will do better. This means the rules are fair and understood by all. Here are some guidelines for when the children visit:

- Children are to be welcomed into your home.
- You and your husband decide on house rules.

- You must explain the rules gently to the children in a kind and loving way so they understand them. This situation is new for them as well. They too are in a transition, and, furthermore, their world has changed dramatically. Look at it from their viewpoint. Their father no longer lives with them, he has left their mother, and he has a new wife.
- Consequences for breaking rules should be known in advance. In that way, they are not punishments because they are known and involve a choice, which has been clearly explained. Punishment, on the other hand, is an angry response, doesn't teach responsibility, and can lead to a power struggle.
- Children must have a place to sleep and play or study in your home.
- You and your husband should meet with the children to discuss weekend plans.
- Children are to be treated respectfully.
- You do not "bad-mouth" their mother.
- You follow through on requests from the mother and rules she makes about her children's care.
- Do not become competitive with their mother for their affection. You cannot replace her and should not try.
- Be cautious and use good taste regarding any physical affection you and your husband show each other in front of the children.

The children may be angry at the change in their lives and may hold you responsible. But you should expect respectful behavior from them even though they may resent you. Your job is to make their visits as pleasant as possible.

Adult Children

If he has adult children, do not assume that the end of their parents' marriage, as well as the affair that led to it, didn't cause them pain. You must treat them respectfully and allow them time to heal their wounds. The guidelines are the same: use good communications skills, and if difficulties arise, use your "I" statements with them and their father whenever it is appropriate. You will have the opportunity to spend more time with the children if they are young than if they are adults. This means younger children have more time to get to know you.

One of the difficulties with older children is that you can become caught up in a power struggle with them. You have the choice to try to find a way to make it work rather than entering into a power struggle.

Your Children

If you are a single mom or have left your husband to marry your lover, your children, too, will have to make an adjustment to the new circumstances. Judith Wallerstein has done long-term studies on the effects of divorce on children and has found that many children are profoundly affected at the time. For many, this becomes a factor in their relationships with the opposite sex as they grow older. Many factors enter into their adjustment, including age and gender.

If you have young children, then your children and his children will become a blended family. One of the issues his children must adjust to concerns the father going to live with another family. A second important change to keep in mind is the birth order of the children in each family as they come together.

There can be competition between the children of each family. For example, in the two families, the oldest child in one may feel displaced if he is no longer the oldest after your marriage. There could be competition between the oldest of each family for that coveted position. The same is true of the youngest. Competition may occur when two children have received recognition for the same achievements, or if one is very deficient in the area where another excels. There are many issues to be aware of, but there are also resources for you to read in the library and online to help you successfully navigate this transition.

The following are some concepts to keep in mind:

- Your children must be told that the changes are not their fault.
- Nothing they did caused theses changes and nothing they do will reverse them.
- Do not use terms like "big happy family" because that is most likely not their experience. They will not feel understood because they probably see it differently.

- Try to understand their feelings, which may include resentment at you and your new husband.
- Respect the loyalty they feel to their father.
- Let them know their father will always be involved in their lives.
- Do everything you can to reduce the impact this change has on their lives.
- Be concrete so that they know when they will see their father and the new rules of their lives.
- Let them know about plans for the holidays, vacations, birthdays, and school events.

Getting Off to a Good Start

I know you would like to get off to a good start, and you know you may run into difficulties because of your affair. In addition to just two people living together with the day-to-day routine of married life, you must now adjust to each other's idiosyncrasies (and everybody has them). Life together will definitely be different from how it was previously in your affair. There are routines that you can incorporate into your life to make the adjustment easier.

Togetherness Time

With the frantic pace in which life is now lived, it is not too hard to imagine that there are couples who do not connect with each other and know what is going on each other's lives, what they are concerned about, and what desires they have. By establishing certain routines, it is possible to build your new world together. This can be done with ease just by talking with each other regularly over a predinner drink, dinner, or dessert. This time is used to focus on each other's day, books you are reading, the news, or anything that has caught your interest. It is a time to know each other better, not a time to read the mail or newspaper or watch television. Even though you may have spent much time together, you may not really have gotten to know each other's deepest beliefs and feelings.

What you will be trying to achieve is a quiet and pleasant time together. This "togetherness time" means you do not discuss family issues or problems. It is not the time to bring up your hurt over how his children may have treated you, your anger at his wife for something, or why you should or shouldn't go to a family event. These issues need to be discussed, but not at this time. They may be inflammatory and the idea is for both of you to be comfortable and know you will not be getting into those problem areas at this time.

Family Meetings

This is a regularly scheduled meeting to review plans for the week, discuss future plans, and address family concerns. It is the time to discuss problems about the relationship with his children and wife or issues that stem from living together. I recommend the family meeting for most couples and families. I believe they should be regularly scheduled once a week on the same day, and should last from a half-hour to an hour. Try not to change the day of the meeting unless something very important comes up, and then immediately reschedule. Each person must give his or her complete attention to the discussion.

This meeting will help reduce tensions as you transition into your new life. There will be fewer arguments during the week because you now know you will have a regularly scheduled time to address issues and to be heard. If you find that there are too many issues to attend to, as there might be in the beginning of your marriage, start with two meetings a week and reduce them to one as the stresses are reduced.

Here are some guidelines that will make the meetings go more smoothly.

Communication Guidelines

1. Do not attack, describe.
    Attack: "You don't give a damn about me. Your daughter, Karen, is more important than I am. I should have known that." (Note: This is also a cognitive distortion called mind reading, which we will discuss shortly.)

Description: "You canceled our dinner plans at the last minute to take your daughter out."

You can see how his response will probably differ:

Response to an attack: "Well, she is important and you just better get used to it."

Response to a description: "My daughter called me very upset about our marriage. I needed to address her concerns. I am sorry. I realize it would have been better if I explained this when I canceled. I can see why you are upset. I feel everybody in the family is important. No one is more or less important than the other." (Note: Her anger will most likely dissipate because she feels understood.)

2. Try to use "I" statements and "I" positions, which are those sentences discussed previously beginning with "I" rather than "you." The former states your preference and the later is used rarely and only on extremely important issues to define your position.
3. Take turns presenting your issue or problem.
4. Listen carefully and show that you are doing so.
5. Respond to what was said, try to use an "I" statement, and show appreciation for your spouse's position. You will have your turn to bring up issues as well.
6. Use "time out" if needed. "Time out" is something like the bell during a boxing match. Each person goes to his or her corner. But the similarity stops here. In families, "time out" gives each person a chance to cool down and think and not come back ready for a fight. In families, "time out" is used when anger rises and a person feels overwhelmed and out of control. When you start this process and review the guidelines, be sure that you understand and agree to use "time out." If you do not agree to this in advance, time out may be perceived as a rejection or abandonment.

This is an example of a time out:

I'm furious. I can't think straight. I need a time out. Let's see how I feel in an hour. I'm going for a walk.

Using the communication skills from Chapter 7, "Assessing Your Affair," will help you as the two of you negotiate this new boundary with his children and his former wife.

Boundaries

Establishing boundaries that all can understand is important for everyone involved. You and your husband will need to agree on the boundaries regarding all your relationships and the role you will play in family events. As his new wife, if he is invited to family events, you should accompany him. If you do not, then you will feel that his family is colluding with his ex-wife, and you are being left out. If there are children, there will be future events like religious celebrations. There will also be birthday parties, graduations, and weddings. As his wife, you should be by his side. Your demeanor there is important. It should be low-key and respectful of the event. In their eyes, you have destroyed a marriage, so singing a solo at the mike and dancing all over the dance floor may be perceived as flaunting. You are also sending a message with your behavior. You are saying, "As his wife, I need to be invited, but you can trust me not to cause a scene, not to be flamboyant, and to honor the occasion in a respectful and appropriate manner."

It is seldom that counseling is completed in one session, but I recall just that with Maria.

"I only need to know one thing. I've been divorced from Anthony for six years. We were married for eighteen. He came from a big family who were wonderful and welcomed me with open arms. His sister, Teresa, became my best friend and our friendship has continued even after the divorce. Anthony is getting married next month and although I have been invited to all the family events since the divorce, I am not invited to the wedding. I don't want to go, even though our children will be there. Teresa hardly calls anymore, and she refuses my invitations. My feelings are hurt that Teresa is acting differently now that Anthony is to be married. What should I expect? Will our friendship end or can it continue after Anthony's married?"

Although no affair was involved in Maria's divorce from Anthony, a transition has occurred and new boundaries are being formed. If Teresa and Maria maintain their friendship, it may seem to Anthony and his new wife that Teresa is being disloyal. Although the family cares about and loves Maria, it is now time to establish a new boundary. I felt this was a loss for Maria and that she needed to talk more about it, but she said that she didn't, and that she had a feeling their friendship could not continue.

> "I have really pulled myself together since the divorce. I have a new life that I really love. I would have liked to continue my friendship with Teresa, but it can't work with a new sister-in-law in the family."

Unfortunately, Teresa was unable to communicate her feelings to Maria. Communication is important to clear the air, to keep people from making erroneous assumptions, and to keep molehills from becoming mountains. But there are land mines out there in the communication field and you need to be aware of them.

Dr. Gottman's "Four Horseman of the Apocalypse"

In his book *The Seven Principles for Making Marriage Work,* Dr. John Gottman identifies what he calls the "Four Horseman of the Apocalypse" that can cause havoc in a marriage. They appear in the way couples communicate with each other. They interfere with understanding, problem-solving, and respect for one another. Dr. Gottman shows us time and again how respect is one of the most important aspects of a good marriage.

The Four Horsemen to be aware of are criticism, defensiveness, contempt, and stonewalling.

Criticism

One very effective way to reduce criticism in communicating, especially on a hot topic, is to use the "I" statement. Picture yourself pointing your finger at yourself and describe how you feel. Then picture yourself pointing your finger at your spouse and starting off by saying "you." The latter is almost guaranteed to end badly. Instead of listening, he will be waiting, if he is able to contain himself, for you to finish so that he can defend himself because he is under attack.

Defensiveness

Criticism leads, of course, to defensiveness. This means that somewhere along the line, he stopped listening and you may be in for a free-for-all. Your feelings or concerns are pushed right out of the picture, because your spouse is reacting to the criticism and will put his efforts into defending himself, rather than listening, understanding, and finding a compromise. He will most likely become aggressive in his style of communication and you may be the recipient of an angry, loud, and frightening response. This is not effective communication! This is yelling at each other and hurting each other's feelings.

Contempt

This is, of course, a putdown that can be very destructive to one's self-esteem, not to mention to the relationship. I think of the brain like a computer that can retrieve those words at any time, and so they go on hurting long after they have been said. It is hard to permanently delete them. On the other hand, when you hear words of encouragement and appreciation, they too stay and are always retrievable as well.

Stonewalling

Stonewalling is used to avoid a conversation or to not take responsibility for one's behavior. It is frustrating to the spouse who wants to be heard, and if it is a chronic problem that needs to be addressed, it is avoided. Not talking about the issue doesn't make it go away; it allows it to fester. The partner bringing up the issue will feel that he or she is not being understood, but most of all he or she is not being respected. As Dr. Gottman points out, "eventually one partner tunes out." The issue is that she feels she has little impact on what goes on in her married life. She is not being allowed to influence her spouse. She might as well not be there. Dr. Gottman believes that being able to influence one another is an extremely important aspect of a good marriage.

Expectations

One of the problems that can arise in a second marriage is that one or both of the individuals may have difficulty in detaching from a former spouse. This can happen even though he or she feels the new marriage is the right choice. An example of such a situation is seen in Anne Tyler's novel *The Amateur Marriage,* in which the long and difficult marriage of Michael and Pauline ends in divorce. After Michael's divorce from Pauline, he continued to help her with automobile checkups, house repairs, and shoveling snow. Even though he had remarried, he was unable to emotionally detach from Pauline. In this novel, his new wife didn't seem to mind, but that is not always the case in real life. This situation often occurs in cases of divorce where the man mows his ex-wife's lawn each week or continues to balance the checkbook. This is due to the difficulty they are having in severing their attachment to each other.

Knowing that the process of detaching emotionally takes time will make you more understanding. The key to success is observing if progress is being made in the process of detaching from a former spouse and to use your communication skills to effectively state your concerns when necessary.

Infidelity Contract

In Chapter 4, there was a quiz called "The Infidelity Danger Zone" to help you try to ascertain the likelihood of your new husband cheating on you. This is usually a major concern for the woman who has married a man who was not faithful to his former wife. You could both have reason not to trust the other, and you may not be sure of his view. British sociologist Annette Lawson found there were fewer incidents of infidelity with couples who had discussions prior to marriage of their expectations on this subject.

It is a good idea to share your views in a conversation devoted solely to this topic. In our book, *Infidelity on the Internet,* Marlene Maheu and I present the idea of couples having this discussion and creating a contract so that each clearly understands the other. For example, some people are confused about what constitutes an affair. Your husband might not consider a relationship on the Internet an affair because there is no touching; you will recognize it as an affair, and so consider it a type of infidelity. The contract involves making a pledge of fidelity according to the way you and he understand it, based on your discussion of the subject. It also includes a promise of honesty and an agreement to share anything that you may feel is a threat to your marriage. For example, if you are working with someone closely at work and are having intrusive thoughts about that person, that should be shared. You have the means to do this at your family meeting.

You now have many of the skills and knowledge needed to manage your new life together. The battle is over. You have won. The true victor is the one who will assume the responsibility of trying to bring peace to the wounded.

Chapter Ten

If the Affair Ends

*S*ometimes you can tell an affair is ending. The signs are there for you to see, but other times it seems to come out of the blue. The way an affair ends depends on a number of factors. You or he may decide independently or jointly to end the relationship, or the affair may have been discovered by his wife, quickly ending it. There are many reasons and scenarios for how an affair ends.

Just as there are many reasons, there are many emotions involved. You may also experience loneliness, not only because you miss him, but also because you may have cut yourself off from family and friends to keep the romance a secret or so you would be available whenever he called. You will probably feel anger or even rage over his treatment of you and the outcome of the affair. There are many emotions you may experience. This chapter is about how to heal.

It's Not Working

His wife's discovery may be the reason, or it could just as easily be an excuse for ending an affair that either one of you feels is not going quite right. The end may come because one or both of you are ambivalent and at last the reason for the ambivalence is understood. Somewhere along the line one of you realizes that it is not working or that it can never work.

You may have mistaken the relationship for a romantic love affair because of his behavior, but for him the affair was a fling. Sometimes this is discussed and the couple agrees that the relationship should end.

It doesn't always end just then. It can take time to process what has happened. So the couple may continue to see each other and gradually drift apart, or they say they are going to try to make changes. They make some, but parts of the relationship keep them from sustaining their intentions.

One or the other of you may feel you do not have as much in common as you first thought. Maybe it is simply that the passion is gone. Or the intimacy needed to sustain a relationship might not have ever developed, or too much intimacy may have developed, making one or both of you uncomfortable. Sometimes, guilt begins to nag at one or the other, or the initial reasons for having the affair no longer exist. It can be one reason or it may be a combination of reasons. But it seems that circumstances have been presented to say adieu.

A Move out of the Area

Sometimes the reasons for ending the affair are clear-cut. Affairs can end when you, your lover, his wife, or (if you are married) your husband moves from the area. A job promotion, a transfer, or a relocation can make the affair difficult, if not impossible, to maintain. Circumstances and true feelings will determine if the affair continues or not. If the distance is great, then it may not be possible to continue seeing each other. Couples sometimes try to cope with the distance but find it difficult unless the new job requires that he or she travel back to the lover's area on some sort of regular basis.

Lifestyle

Either one or the other of the pair may end the affair because the secrecy and planning involved in their lifestyle becomes too much of a burden.

> *Leslie:* "My husband was getting suspicious of my extra meetings at work, and so I gave Larry an ultimatum, and he said that it's his way or the highway. That hurt. So I'm taking the highway. I've had it."

Sometimes couples discuss this issue and try to work it out.

Lucy: "Even though I love him and wanted more than anything to marry him, I've come to believe it may not happen and I cannot go on with hiding and lying. I am close to accepting that. I especially feel bad when I lie to my mother. I don't have a life. I just stick around waiting for him to fit me into his schedule. We had a talk and he promised he would try to make more advance plans and not act as though I should always just be there. Things are just not falling into place."

Lucy says she is close to accepting the fact that they will not marry and feels she is only asking for more consideration. However, she is really testing the waters about the prospect of marriage. Lucy is discovering that ending the affair is more difficult to do than she had anticipated. She wants to end the affair because her lover is having difficulty adjusting his life to meet her needs, and her requests are becoming a constant source of friction between them. It may be that he does not really want to adjust his lifestyle or that he cannot. If he wants an affair and not a marriage, it may be that this is all the time he wants to devote to the affair. At this point in a relationship many women come to the conclusion that leaving may be the better solution, and so they, like Lucy, make the decision to end the affair.

Discovery

When someone has discovered the affair, the relationship could end immediately. The reaction of the faithful spouse could tip the balance of the ambivalence that either party feels, as well as the underlying feelings about the affair.

Lori: "Things have been horrible in my house since Lawrence found out. It's for the best that this affair is over. I've had bad feelings about what I was doing. I want to make it right. Now's my chance."

Janet: "It just wasn't worth all that pain. I was not up to the drama."

Neil: "When I saw Paula's reaction when she found out about Michele, I never felt so much guilt. It was hard because I had very tender feelings for Michele, but I had no idea that this would hurt Paula the way it did. The affair is over, but not the consequences. I live with it every day."

These people voice reactions that the fight for the affair wasn't worth it. Some women want the wife to find out, believing that will bring it out in the open and lead to a resolution. Calling the wife on the phone is a long shot, but the chance of it backfiring is not—it is very likely to happen.

Ashley: "I called his wife and I told her what was going on. She was shocked, but I told her I would fight for him. He was furious. He took her side and he ended it."

What Ashley didn't realize is that, despite the pain and shock, most wives will rally for the continuation of their marriage, and so will the lover.

The Triangle Becomes More Complicated

One reason affairs end is that another person attracts the attention of one of the lovers. It can happen to anyone in the triangle. You could meet another man whom you find sexually attractive or intriguing and want to explore a relationship with him, or it could be that your lover has found a new love and ends the affair. The wife may also have an affair, or the husband of a married woman may do the same.

Many women report the shock they experienced when told that their lover was leaving his wife—to marry someone else! He evidently wasn't ambivalent about the affair. He just wasn't honest with his lover about his feelings. He wanted the affair, but did not want to marry his lover.

Affairs of retaliation on the part of the husband are "leaked." After all, this is the point of an affair of retaliation. It is done to hurt the spouse, and the only way for that to happen is to make the affair known to his wife. Although this is not as common as other reasons, it does happen and it shakes things up. The affair ends, unless he finds himself enjoying the affair and decides to change his course of action.

He Passes His Test

There are times when the man has an affair to test his abilities to attract another woman and to experience another relationship. He may have thought at some point that he might want to leave his marriage, but is not completely sure. The affair becomes a testing ground for him about whether this is the right step. If he enjoys the time away from his wife and can attract another woman who appreciates him, he may decide to leave his marriage. It doesn't necessarily mean he is in love with his lover; it just means he passed the test. She has been used as a transitional person to the next stage of his life.

If he has tested his ability to attract another woman, he will most likely find the excitement of the affair and the rise in self-esteem very positive. If he has problems at home and not in the affair, he may believe another woman will be the answer to his needs. Or the affair may seem to ease his own problems that have nothing to do with the marriage and everything to do with him. He may find that the solution he believes came from the affair may fade in time, just as it did with his marriage. This is another reason to know the lover well before marrying him. He, of course, may not be aware of the distinction between marriage and an affair. When an affair becomes a marriage, his problems may return.

Cold Feet

Sometimes an affair ends because one of the lovers has doubts, guilt, or becomes anxious over the relationship. The man may feel it is going too fast and he is too pressured by his lover to continue in a direction and at a speed he does not want.

She, on the other hand, may get cold feet when he is ready to leave his marriage. This is what she always wanted, and now she can't go through with it. What has happened? There can be a number of reasons, but the most obvious is that the unavailable man is now available. If, in her unconscious, he is a substitute for her father, the anxiety can rise and the ensuing guilt may be intolerable. She cannot go through with it. The heartbreak of ending the affair is more tolerable than the guilt.

Even if the relationship breaks up over a period of time or fizzles out, the sense of loss can still be acute. This can be especially true if it ends acrimoniously.

Can't We Just Be Friends?

Sometimes the man wants to remain a friend after the affair is concluded. This usually happens when he is considerably older than his lover. Andrew Morton reports in his book *Monica's Story* that President Clinton told Monica that he could be a friend. Some women are able to remain friends with their lover, while others are not.

In Marie Brenner's collection of profiles of famous older women, *Great Dames*, she details the life of Pamela Harriman. At the end of Harriman's life, she was the American ambassador to France. She died a month before her seventy-seventh birthday from a cerebral hemorrhage after swimming in the pool at the Ritz Hotel in Paris.

Even though Pamela Harriman is not the typical woman, she is important to our understanding of our subject because she had many lovers who were very powerful men, and many of them were married. Their wives knew of the affairs, as did all of their friends. Some well-known lovers were CBS newscaster Edward R. Murrow and millionaire Averill Harriman. These particular affairs occurred while she was married to Randolph Churchill, son of Prime Minister Winston Churchill. By that time, Pamela was an international figure traveling in the high society of Europe and the United States. When her relationship with Averill Harriman ended, they continued to be friends and she accepted "a monthly stipend from him for the next thirty years." The stipend ended when she married him. Harriman was twenty-nine years older than Pamela. She is an example of a woman who was able to remain "friends" with her ex-lovers. Many powerful married men help support their lover financially in some way. Some help with college expenses and

some later become their mentors. It depends on the couple and the individual circumstances whether they can remain friends.

Talk of Marriage

If you came to believe that marriage was in your future from promises
that were made, your reaction at the end of the affair will include disappointment and a feeling of betrayal.

> *Beth:* "I feel as though I've been duped. We talked of our marriage
> and he allowed me to dream about it. It was hard to believe that he
> would be so specific, when he really had no intention of following
> through."

Some men know that they will not leave their wives, and they are
just leading their lover on. Others believe they may marry, but when the
cards are on the table, they find they aren't able to leave their wife. This
for many men is the time they think through the consequences, and
decide their marriage comes first.

> *Beth:* "He told me he had really believed he could marry me, but
> his feeling for his wife was stronger than he thought. In fact, stron-
> ger than I thought."

The couple that talks of marriage, because they are both experiencing a romantic love affair, may or may not marry. Those who do
not marry for whatever reason have a difficult time recovering from a
breakup, because the man is sincere in wanting to marry his lover. She
comes very close to being his wife. They part because one or both feel
unable to continue in the present situation if they cannot marry.

The man who is having a romantic love affair and wants to marry
his lover, but does not, takes the breakup badly and goes through a rough
period. He is depressed and must work through his depression. If his
wife doesn't know about the affair, he must make excuses for his sadness
and withdrawal. It is difficult to conceal a depression from someone you
are living with. But it is a bumpy road for the man when his wife knows

why he is depressed. His wife watches his reaction in despair while she is simultaneously struggling with her rage and feelings of betrayal.

It is difficult to leave when you are in love. In the film *Closer,* Daniel Wolf (Jude Law) says to Alice (Natalie Portman) with surprise, "You mean you never left someone you still love?" There are times when the evidence shows the affair may not work, and ending it even though you are still in love, may be the right choice.

At this point, you may have the answer to your question. He may not want to leave his family. You may have to give up someone you love. If he is not a responsible partner or he is not willing to marry you, then you have the power to leave the relationship. You then can take charge of your own life. Your future is in your hands and you have the power to change it and make it what you would like. You have choices and because of that you are empowered. You are no longer a lady-in-waiting.

Reactions to an Ending

It is painful to end a relationship to which you have given so much of yourself and in which you expected so much from your lover. There are many losses involved of which you are keenly aware. Perhaps the most searing pain is the loss of your dreams. The reactions to loss are similar to grief such as shock, disbelief, anger, depression, and finally acceptance. It is also similar to the reactions to a transition.

Depression

A depressed person experiences profound sadness, crying spells, changes in sleeping and eating habits, a loss of pleasure in previously enjoyed activities, and difficulties in cognitive functioning like memory and concentration. It is hard to get started in the morning and small things can bring on a crying spell. Hearing a favorite song on the radio, shopping in the market and seeing one of his favorite foods, or being alone on one of the regularly scheduled times you used to spend together can make you sad. The depression should begin to lift gradually. If you feel your depression is worsening or you see no improvement, if you cannot function at work or at home, or if you have any thoughts about harming yourself, then you must contact a mental health professional or go to your nearest emergency room for help. Even though you feel as badly as you do, you must remember that depression is treatable.

There are some very effective self-help measures that can aid in lifting your depression. There are many definitions of depression, but the way cognitive therapists view depression dovetails with the definition of a *transition* that we have been discussing. A cognitive definition gives us a tool to use in combating the depression. Cognitive therapists look at depression as a negative view of your world, yourself, your future. The word *view* tells us that it is concerned with how we think about the events that happen to us. It is our interpretation of the events. Cognitive therapists explain that depression and anxiety are related to distorted thinking.

Distorted Thinking

Since thoughts determine our feelings, we need to check our thinking to see if there are any distortions in thought that can help account for the way we feel. Although we understand the source of sadness, we need to challenge any distortions in thought to see if that is adding to the sadness. This also relates to our concept of fusion of thoughts and feelings. The challenge is to separate thinking from feeling by looking at the facts and seeing if you have used any cognitive distortions that worsen the depression. We then can reduce the level of depression that such thinking may exacerbate.

Cognitive distortions are a form of distorted thinking. The following ten cognitive distortions are listed in the book *Feeling Good* by Dr. David Burns. You will see how faulty thinking can raise the level of emotional reactivity. In these examples, the distortion is explained and an example of its use is shown. Following each is a statement that challenges the distortion and shows another way of thinking that is not distorted. This concept can be applied to many situations. Some people tend to use one or more distortions on a regular basis. Understanding them and being observant about how you use them will help you now and in your future.

1. **All or nothing thinking:** This describes a way of looking at situations in extremes. It has been called "black or white thinking." It does not allow for moderation.

   Distortion: "Ted is my soul mate. If I can't have him, there is no joy in my life."
   Change to: "I loved Ted and losing him is very painful, but I will find ways to heal my pain and create a satisfying life."

   Despair can be changed to hope even though you feel the pain from the situation.

2. **Overgeneralization:** This occurs when a person takes one event and paints it with a broad stroke to include everything.

   Distortion: "He is the only person that I can be happy with."
   Change to: "I was happy with him, but he is not the only guy in the world. There are others. I will have to meet them and find out if I can be happy with others."

   In the change of statement, the individual does not wipe out her future by saying every other person will pale in comparison to her lover.

3. **Mental filter:** This happens when one event among many is focused on and all others lose significance.

   Distortion: "He was a man who had everything—looks, personality, and sex appeal."
   Change to: "He had a lot of admirable traits, but he also was a liar and a cheat."

4. **Disqualifying the positive:** This refers to a pessimistic reading of positive events that happen, but you believe they just don't count. "Beginners luck" is an example of how many positive attributes can quickly be discounted.

   Distortion: "I'm not the sort of woman who attracts men. It was just a fluke that Benny cared about me."
   Change to: "It wasn't just a fluke. I do have something going for me that can attract men."

5. **Jumping to Conclusions:** Making an assumption about someone's behavior or motivation and not checking it out with that person puts you in the category of mind reading or fortune telling.

   Mind reading:
   Distortion: "Everyone will think poorly of me for being involved with a married man."
   Change to: "Maybe they will. I don't know that people even spend that much time thinking about me. I also have no idea what they think unless they tell me or I ask them. I can only change my behavior."

   Related to this is predicting the future. This is also referred to as "fortune telling."

   Fortune telling:
   Distortion: "I just keep making one mistake after the other. I am sure the next time I fall in love it will end just as badly as all the others."
   Change to: "I wanted him to love me so badly that I ignored all the signs that indicated he didn't. In my next relationship, I will not become involved with a married man and I will look for signs of his intentions."

   This, as you can see, is based on the same principle as mind reading because it is coming to conclusions without any evidence to support it. However, when you state it correctly, you do not deny your reality, and challenging your distorted thinking shows your future looks more promising. You can see how this will lower emotional reactivity and decrease the feeling of hopelessness because you have identified a starting point for change.

6. **Minimization/magnification:** These are distortions that take a sledgehammer to your self-esteem by minimizing your achievements and magnifying your errors.

   Distortion: "No one will care that I manage some major portfolio for the bank where I work. They will only care that I had an affair with a married man."
   Change to: "I will focus on my professional achievements and be proud of them. An affair with a married man was a mistake that I regret."

7. **Emotional reasoning:** This distortion refers to the tendency to attribute conclusions to the way you feel. It is a really important distortion to recognize and give up if you have been using it.

   Distortion: "I feel like a failure. He seemed so in love with me and I did not see that he really wasn't."
   Change to: "The relationship failed because he was married and cared about his wife. I am not a failure, but I am concerned about what I did. I've learned a lot."

8. **Should statement:** This distortion sets standards that you compare behavior to, whether it is yours or someone else's. It can lead to guilt. In many cases, the guilt can be changed to regret.

   Distortion: "I should have seen how badly he treated all the other women in his life."
   Change to: "I regret I didn't see how badly he treated other women, but I have learned a lesson from that."

9. **Labeling and mislabeling:** This amounts to a one-word critique that does not allow a deeper and more accurate description of a person or an event. An example of this would be recognizing that a colleague's pressure at work and at home could account for his behavior. Rather than label him a jerk, trying to be more understanding of the situation is the better course of action. Applying labels to yourself is similar. Rather than label yourself, describe the situation.

   Distortion: "I was such an idiot to think he loved me."
   Change to: "I wanted so badly for him to love me that I ignored all the signs that indicated he didn't."

10. **Personalization:** This is a distortion in which a person sees herself as responsible for events that were not her fault.

    Distortion: "I'm responsible for their marriage falling apart."
    Change to: "I take responsibility for causing stress in their marriage, but I cannot take responsibility for it falling apart. He also was a partner to the affair and neither one would seek counseling when they were aware of their marital problems. We all played a part."

The Things You Tell Yourself

We have another excellent tool for challenging our thinking. Cognitive therapist Dr. Albert Ellis, the originator of Rational Emotive Behavior Therapy, tells us that we feel the way we think. The problem lies in the "sentences" we say to ourselves. He has provided us with a simple formula to help us get to the bottom of it. The formula is A + B = C:

A is the *activating* event and it is objective.
It has happened; it is a fact.
B is your *belief* about A. It is subjective.
This is the cause of our disturbing emotions.
C is the (emotional) *consequence.*

After we experience the emotional consequences that are easily detected because we say or think something and then feel depressed, guilty, or anxious, Dr. Ellis tells us to apply his formula of A + B = C. At that point, we look at what happened or what we thought or said (A), and then we check our belief system (B) for any irrational thoughts (that is, the sentences we tell ourselves). He calls the last part of the process "D," which stands for *dispute.* At this point, we must challenge the validity of our belief (B). Here's how it works:

A: The affair is ending.
B: This is the worst thing that could ever happen to me.
C: You feel depressed.
D: It is not the worst thing that could happen. You may be feeling badly about it, but there are worse things that could happen such as ill health and death. It is regrettable from your standpoint and you have learned a lot from this experience. You may also recognize that the belief (B) expressed in this example is a cognitive distortion "All or Nothing Thinking."

You can help yourself reduce the degree of emotional consequences like depression, guilt, despair, and anxiety by keeping a daily diary of when you experience those feelings. Then note what you may have been thinking right before that. It may be a "sentence" that you said to yourself that resulted in those disturbing emotions. Next, apply Dr. Ellis's formula of A + B = C, or use Dr. Burns's ten cognitive distortions to challenge your thinking. The result will be not only be a change in the degree of emotional reactivity, but a step toward separating your thinking from your emotional process.

Obsessive Review

Along with depression, one of the most troubling reactions is the obsessive review. When traumatic events occur in our lives, there is a tendency to review them over and over again. Psychiatrist Robert Weiss wrote about this in *Marital Separation* because most divorcing individuals usually engage in this mental review. When an affair is revealed, it is a catastrophic event for the wife. She finds it unbelievable and unacceptable, and this causes her to go over and over it in her mind. It really is an obsession. You can be sure that if his wife knows about you, she is reviewing her marriage, the clues that she missed, or the times she thinks you might have been together.

If you have found that the affair is ending or not working out the way you had wanted, you also may be reviewing your time together. You will be searching for the clues that you have missed that showed it would not work out, and for all the events you thought were indications that you could have a future together. The obsessive review is a painful process, but it is done to integrate this event into your life and make it part of your history. Women tell me they feel as though they are going crazy because they can't stop thinking about their affair. They are more relaxed about it when they learn it is an expected reaction and that it will fade away until it is gone. They are not going crazy—it is part of the healing process.

Obsessive reviews have occurred on national and international scales when a traumatic, unexpected event occurs. This will help you understand the nature of the review. For example, older Americans remember the assassination of President John F. Kennedy and the repeated coverage of that tragedy. Many recall the death of Princess Diana and how the nation became totally absorbed with the tragedy. People reviewed the event obsessively from television and reader accounts in magazines and newspapers. The most recent occurrences that caused such an obsessive review were the terrorist attacks on America on September 11, 2001, and the tsunami in

December of 2004, when more than 150,000 people were killed instantly and a similar number were unaccounted for and thought to be dead.

How does one cope with such an obsessive process when it occurs in the context of an affair? The first step is to try to confine your review to a certain time during the day. This way, you can gain control of the obsession. Allow yourself an hour to do your review. The best time is an hour before another activity that must be done. This makes ending your review easier.

How to Review

1. Set the time for about one hour, once a day. If thoughts are intruding throughout the day, you can tell yourself that you will have time to review later. This often works, but if it does not, adjust your schedule to a half-hour, twice a day.
2. Decrease the time and frequency as you see improvement.
3. Be alone with no interruptions.
4. Allow yourself to think about whatever comes to your mind about the affair.
5. Set a timer or have a clock nearby.
6. Do not exceed your predetermined time limit.

Even though you will have a set time to review, thoughts may come to you during the day. There are thought-stopping techniques you can use to keep from starting the review earlier than the set time. Basically, the concept is to signal yourself in some way to stop your obsessive thinking:

- Wear a rubber band on your wrist, and "snap" it whenever such thoughts arise at the wrong time.
- Pinch yourself as a reminder to stop those intrusive thoughts.
- Visualize a Stop sign.
- Pop a mint into your mouth as a signal to stop.

Loneliness

You may be feeling very lonely, but even more than that, you may see yourself as alone. In their book *In Search of Intimacy,* Carin Rubenstein and Phil Shaver describe two types of loneliness and some of the behaviors that can promote or discourage loneliness.

Emotional Loneliness

Loneliness due to a lack of friends or family to provide you with support is *emotional loneliness,* experienced when you do not have another individual with whom to share concerns. This is a person who is with you through thick and thin, someone you can count on, and who is a cherished friend. Ask yourself where your emotional support came from before your affair, and if it is still intact, make contact and share the recent events of your life. Allow your friend to offer emotional support.

Heather: "I can't do that because I never shared this part of my life with Jan. She will be hurt and feel like I was not much of a friend."

Heather's fears may be groundless. She doesn't really know how Jan may react until she talks to her. She is using a cognitive distortion. She is jumping to conclusions without checking out the facts. Jan may well understand Heather's need for secrecy.

Becky: "I can't tell Terri how it ended, because she predicted this would happen."

Even though Terri predicted the ending, it doesn't mean she would not offer support. Becky is jumping to conclusions. Does she have a crystal ball that tells her Terri's reaction? Terri's warning may very well have been a sign of her caring, rather than the "I told you so" attitude Becky predicts.

Sharon: "I have no one to talk to. I never had many friends, and I was so involved with Kent that I just didn't continue keeping up with anyone. I don't want to resume those contacts now."

There are other ways Sharon can find support when there is a need for emotional contact. One option is contacting a therapist who has experience working with couples and working through grief. Another option is finding a support group of women, men and women, or women in transition. Before working with a group, it is a good idea to have a meeting with the group leader to see how you would fit in according to issue, age, and gender. A leader sees that a group runs smoothly, that members are not judgmental, that everyone has a chance to be heard and receive appropriate feedback. The leader sees that boundaries are observed and members respect one another. It often takes a few meetings for a group to become cohesive and caring. The group goes through a process of finding itself and settling down. Ongoing groups have been through that process and can integrate new members. It pays to be patient, because the members reach out to each other in a very positive way. You can see the progress you make by remembering how you felt when you first started in the group and how you feel at a later point.

Another, newer way of finding emotional support is on the Internet, in chat rooms. A chat room can be helpful if you cannot find a therapist or a group. It is best to find an online chat room that is set up in the same way as an offline group. It should have an experienced professional leader, guidelines that govern the group, and strict adherence to rules of confidentiality. A group usually meets once a week for one and a half hours. That is all the time that should be devoted to this kind of support. You must be very careful in your search to find an appropriate chat room for women. Because of the pseudo-intimacy that quickly develops online, you need to pick one that has safeguards and is led by a trained professional. An online chat room should show the same respect for its members as an offline group.

Social Loneliness

Social loneliness occurs when people are isolated from interaction with others. Some aspects of your affair, such as the secrecy or the need to stay at home waiting for a call, may have fostered social loneliness.

When the loneliness that you are experiencing is due to isolation or lack of friends to share activities with, it is worth putting forth the effort to find ways to be in contact with others. These are not people you have to bare your soul to, but individuals who enjoy doing the same things you do. It is social support, not emotional. If a friendship forms it is then based on shared interests.

Social Action

This is a way to change the social isolation that you may be experiencing. There are many ways to meet others. Even though your energy may be low due to depression, now is the time to take a class, pursue an interest, or learn a hobby. Research the classes that are available at your local universities, credit or noncredit. Check out the libraries, museums, and local newspapers. You may find sports activities, book discussion groups, computer classes, concert series, and other interests.

Getting involved is the key to help with the isolation and the self-absorption that accompany a loss. Such involvement can mean volunteering in hospitals, associations, or politics. There are causes in this world that are begging for help. Think of the political or nonprofit organizations, or religious groups that might need your help.

You will also feel less lonely by contacting people by telephone, e-mail, or letters. This is a social contact even though you are not in the presence of that person. The idea is to find people who can become part of your life in a way that you might not have thought of before.

Active Solitude

This is a way to be by yourself and not feel lonely. You can enjoy the time you spend alone by doing activities that are of interest to you, and at the same time you learn something new or increase your skills. The ability to be alone and engaged is called "active solitude." Playing the piano, baking, listening to music, or working with an exercise video are some of the ideas I have heard.

Distraction

There are times when you can use some simple distractions that will ease immediate and intense discomfort. Distraction isn't a long-term solution for emotional or social loneliness, but it can get you through rough spells. Get out of the house to break the mood, even if it is just to take a walk, go to a bookstore, take in a movie, or rent a video. This will help in those disturbing moments. Pamper yourself when needed even if it is only to take a nice hot bubble bath by candlelight and music. These will not solve your problem, but will help you now.

Sad Passivity

There is a group of activities to be avoided, since you don't grow from them and because they usually make you feel worse. This category includes drinking, using drugs, overeating, not eating, crying, or getting into bed and pulling the covers over your head. These are self-destructive behaviors. Sad passivity is like driving a car in reverse. It will take you further and further from your goals and cause you more pain in the long run. Distraction is like putting your car in neutral. You won't get anywhere, but you won't get hurt either. Social action and active solitude are moving forward, self-enhancing, and will take you in the right direction.

Dealing with the End of the Affair

When the affair is over, the resulting emotional turmoil can seem overwhelming. In the previous sections we talked about ways to deal with the very difficult and disconcerting emotions you experience in ending an affair such as depression, anxiety, loneliness, and the obsessive review and presented effective and important strategies and interventions based on solid theoretical thinking so that you can help yourself in recovering from this loss. They deal specifically with these emotions. Now we will look at strategies that are self-soothing, more general, easy to do, and very effective in helping you find relief from the discomfort you are experiencing. You are in a process of mourning, and it is important to have all the tools to deal with it.

Self-Soothing

Whenever you are hurting, you need to engage in behaviors that are self-soothing. It is a way to care for yourself when you are anxious, depressed, or angry.

Journaling

Keeping a journal of your thoughts and feelings can help you with the upsetting emotions you are experiencing. The journal is a way to freely express yourself and ventilate anger. Writing a journal is an outlet for your emotions and is available to you even when no one else is. It is "for your eyes only." There are no rules for journaling. You can write it whenever you feel like it. Some people record their comments on a regular basis, others as they feel the need to do so. There are no grammatical rules to follow—incomplete sentences, phrases, spelling mistakes—all is acceptable. Only you will read it.

It is helpful to date each entry. As you are further along in your journal, you can look back and see the progress you have made. Entries in the beginning of a journal will be different from the later ones. They usually reflect a change in your degree of depression, a lessening of anger, and your integration of this experience into your life.

Most women find the journal a very helpful tool that chronicles their changes. However, a few women find it upsetting to put these thoughts on paper. If you find that this routinely happens with you—stop this exercise. There are other strategies that will help you.

Exercise

Think of anger as a fuel that needs to be burned off. A good way to do this is to have a regular exercise program commensurate with your health and age. Not only will your anger begin to dissipate, but your health and body will benefit as well.

Women have often been advised to burn off anger by "pillow punching," but many women find that this makes them feel angrier than when they started. Again, if this is your experience, stop "pillow punching." If it increases your anger, it is counterproductive.

I remember a woman who did a martial arts routine in which she pretended she was striking her former lover. It helped her, but strategies that help some may not help all.

The Unmailed Letter

Another strategy for reducing your anger is to write your lover a letter expressing your feelings about the affair. For example, if you feel your lover has misled you, put that in your letter. Tell him about your resentment over any poor treatment you feel you received. You can write about waiting for his calls, your loneliness on special occasions, his leading you on, and the times you felt overlooked.

When you finish, read the letter and put it away. DO NOT MAIL IT! DO NOT EVER MAIL IT! Mailing this letter will not cause him to change. It will not bring him back into your life. This letter is for you. It is to help you get relief by expressing your feelings. People are often surprised at how much better they feel after having the freedom to say what they want in the safety of the therapist's office. If you do not have such an opportunity, this letter may do that for you.

When you feel better, read your letter. Then you can perform a ritual that may continue the therapeutic effects of getting this off your chest. Tear the letter into little pieces and flush them away, or—using safety precautions—burn them. Some people have thrown them in the ocean, others have buried them.

Relaxation Techniques

Developing a means of relaxing is helpful during this period. If you have a technique that you are familiar with, this is the time to use it. The benefits to your physical and mental health have long been recognized.

There are general guidelines to follow for effective ways to relax.

- Select a time when you are not rushed and do not expect interruptions.
- Find a quiet comfortable place.
- Sit or lie down.
- Wear comfortable clothing.
- Dim the lights.
- Plan to spend about ten to fifteen minutes for each session.
- The number of sessions depends on your degree of tension. Between one and three is a good starting point. Adjust the frequency according to your needs.
- If you should feel lightheaded or uncomfortable, stop and try again at another time.

Deep breathing
This will make your muscles relax and feel good.

1. Inhale through your nose. The air will enter your body and as it does your chest, rib cage, and abdomen will rise. This will take only two or three seconds.

2. Hold this breath for a count of three seconds.
3. Exhale slowly for a count of six to eight seconds. Your chest, rib cage, and abdomen will return to their normal position.
4. Repeat three times.
5. Notice how relaxed your body feels.

Progressive muscle relaxation

Dr. Edmond Jacobson, a Chicago physician, devised this procedure in 1929. It remains an excellent way to experience a relaxed state. Essentially, muscles are contracted and then released in groups.

1. Contract the muscles on your face, hold for five seconds, and release.
2. Contract the next group of muscles by starting with your fingers and making a fist. Then pull your arms close to your body and tighten your muscles. Release. Notice how relaxed your muscles feel.
3. Next, contract and hold the muscles of your trunk and then release. Once again, notice how relaxed these muscles feel.
4. Finally, contract and hold the muscles of your buttocks, thighs, legs, and feet. Release. Once again, notice how relaxed these muscles feel.

Visualization

Imagining a peaceful scene can be a very effective means of relaxing. It helps to put on soft music. The essence of this technique is to use your imagination to create a calming scene. Start by breathing deeply and closing your eyes. The following is my favorite visualization.

Imagine you are walking through a beautiful meadow. You notice the pastel wild flowers in bloom as you walk by. It is very pleasant. The sun is shining and you feel very comfortable and relaxed. You are enjoying yourself. You come to a lake and you admire its beauty. You turn to the right and you see logs slowly floating down a stream. Soon they are in front of you and you watch as they pass you. You notice that as they go down the stream, they become smaller and smaller until you cannot see them anymore. After a few seconds, you turn and walk back through the meadow. Once again you notice the beautiful flowers.

Open your eyes, stretch, and notice that you feel very relaxed.

A variation on this visualization is to imagine balloons floating away and becoming smaller until you cannot see them.

Rituals

When you are experiencing a transition, it is like closing one door and opening another. It is hard, at times, to close the door to the past and to open a new door if there is uncertainty about what you will find. In life we experience a series of transitions, and for many, there is a ritual that helps us leave one experience and enter the next. We say "goodbye" with rituals like graduation and bachelor parties, and with final farewells, we memorialize the life of a loved one with a service. We start a new beginning with a wedding ceremony, a bridal shower, or a housewarming.

Some transitions lack rituals, but people are developing them because they feel the emotional need to mark the event and to be able to move forward. Some people have created rituals for leaving a marriage and a home. Recognizing the significance of these events helps us to successfully negotiate these transitions.

The end of an affair has no ritual, but one can be created. It is one that may have to be done alone because of the nature of the affair. In *The Pilot's Wife*, we see such a ritual when Kathryn visits the area where her husband's plane went down. The boat she takes goes directly to the spot where the cockpit was found. She looks at the water and is silent for a while and then says, "Goodbye, Jack." She completes her ritual as she slowly releases the ring from her hand and watches it disappear into its watery grave.

Most rituals have someone who bears witness to the occasion, as in graduations or funerals, but this does not necessarily have to be. If a friend or family member knows of the affair and you feel comfortable with them, they can be with you at the time of your ritual. Some of the most moving rituals I have heard are from women who have created their own ritual and done it alone.

You too can create a ritual to use when you are ready to let go of the resentment and close the book on this part of your life. Burn your unmailed letter to symbolize "burning your bridges," bury it to represent letting go, flush it away or send it down a stream in torn pieces to symbolize washing him away. You will have said goodbye.

I know of people who have donated books on topics of comfort or inspiration to a library or an institution as a way of saying goodbye. The one rule of doing rituals is to do no harm. Do not involve his wife, children, or anyone connected with him. If you desire to involve them, then you are not ready to say goodbye or to perform the ritual. This ritual is for you and it is a way to say goodbye and bring you peace. You will be ready to open a new door and explore a new world.

Restructuring Your Life

You must restructure your life and your thinking to accommodate this new set of assumptions about yourself, your life, and your world after the end of the affair. Transitions, you may remember, can be stressful.

Other things will change as well. Gone will be all the situations that perturbed you, embarrassed you, or made you angry. There will be no more waiting hours or days for a phone call, no more wondering where he is, and no more having to live life in the shadows.

Along with the stress over the loss of your lover and your dreams of your future together, there may be anxiety about life without him and what your future may bring. The routine of life will change. You will not have the regularly scheduled events to look forward to, and those particular times will seem especially empty. It is a time of missing him. You will also miss his passion and his delight at being with you.

Moving Forward

The question you may now be struggling with is how you pick up the pieces and continue with your life. First, you must realize that this is a process and that it doesn't end because the affair is over. Earlier I wrote about the initial reactions of shock, anger, depression, and the obsessive review. To reach the point of acceptance and to move forward with your life, there are other stages, which B. Hopson and J. Adams describe in their chapter, "Toward an Understanding of Transitions: Defining Some Boundaries of Transition," in the text *Transitions: Understanding and Managing Personal Change:*

1. Shock and immobilization
2. Denial
3. Depression
4. Letting go
5. Testing options
6. Integration

Since we have already discussed the initial reactions of the transition, we are now ready to take the next step, which is *Letting go.* You are ready to let go of the past and this experience. You will find any resistance to change disappearing. The next step is *Testing Options,* which is a critical point when you are ready to face a new challenge. It is a search for opportunities. At this point, you prepare yourself for your new life by contacting friends, developing new interests, or trying out long-desired plans. As this is developed, you will find you are now at the end of the transition and in the *Integration* phase, where you are ready to make this part of your history and get on with your life. Most importantly, the authors found that self-esteem is *higher* at the end of a transition than at the beginning. Imagine yourself as a new free person with a smorgasbord before you to create a life you would like.

The most important benefit of all from this experience is the process of finding who you are, that deep within you will be the gift to be all that you can be. Your spirits can soar. And then you are free to create a life of your own design unfettered by longings from the past. Open to you will be the appropriate available man and a life of your own creation.

This will be possible because in the words of poet Sara Teasdale, in her poem "On The South Downs":

> *It was not you, though you were near,*
> *Though you were good to hear and see;*
> *It was not the earth, it was not heaven,*
> *It was myself that sang in me.*

Appendix

Form for Assessing Your Affair

A. About You

The Situation

_____

_____

_____

_____

How do you experience the affair on the continuum?

❏ Serial

❏ Fling

❏ Romantic

❏ Long-term affair

Stressors previous to the affair

_____

_____

_____

_____

Current stressor

_____

_____

_____

_____

Family-of-origin

_____

_____

_____

_____

B. About Him

How does he experience the affair on the continuum?

❏ Serial

❏ Fling

❏ Romantic

❏ Long-term affair

Stressors previous to the affair

_____

_____

_____

_____

Current stressor

_____

_____

_____

_____

Family-of-origin

_____

_____

_____

_____

C. About His Wife

Regardless of how he describes her, what do you believe she is really like?

_____

_____

_____

_____

What evidence is there that she is the way he described her to you?

_____

_____

_____

_____

What power does she have to keep him from leaving her?

_____

_____

_____

_____

D. About the Affair

At what stage is your affair?

❏ Attraction

❏ Honeymoon

❏ Disequilibrium

❏ An answer

What has been happening to your self-esteem?

_____

_____

_____

_____

Do you feel powerless, or not? Explain.

_____

_____

_____

_____

Is your relationship going in the direction you want? Explain.

_____

_____

_____

_____

Does Dr. Richard Tuch's quote apply to you? His statement is, "He has two women, she has half a man." How?

_____

_____

_____

_____

E. Questions

Throughout this book, you were presented with quizzes for self-examination and questions that needed to be answered. Following is an abbreviated list of questions for you to answer.

Is he a poor-risk partner? Explain.

_____

_____

_____

_____

_____

How committed do you believe he is to his marriage?

_____

_____

_____

_____

What evidence supports that belief?

_____

_____

_____

Does he discuss leaving his marriage? _____

What evidence do you have that shows he is serious about leaving?

_____

_____

_____

_____

Does he avoid discussing your future? _____

Does he set dates for leaving and then not leave? _____

What sacrifice is he making for the affair?

_____

_____

_____

_____

What kind of emotional support has he given you when you need it?

_____

_____

_____

_____

What kind of evidence do you have that you can count on him to be there for you in emergencies?

_____

_____

_____

_____

If a child were to be conceived from your relationship, what do you think his reaction would be?

_____

_____

_____

_____

F. A Deeper Look

What are the reasons that led you to have this affair?

❏ Intimacy _____

❏ Loneliness _____

❏ Old flame _____

❏ Tony Soprano syndrome _____

❏ Geographical separation _____

❏ Attraction at close range _____

❏ Transitions _____

❏ Other _____

What are you doing to find a way to resolve the reason, other than an affair?

_____

_____

_____

_____

Are you repeatedly involved with an unavailable man? _____

Could you be assessing his experience as being a romantic love affair when it is a fling? Explain.

_____

_____

_____

_____

Are you sacrificing any goals, needs, wants for the affair?

_____

_____

_____

_____

How would you rate the quality of your life?

_____

_____

_____

_____

Is the affair keeping you from having a fuller, richer life? Explain.

_____

_____

_____

_____

How much time do you want to give to someone who has not been able to commit to you?

_____

_____

Is it better to know now or later?

_____

How will you feel three, five, fifteen years from now if the answer to your question "Will he really leave her for me?" is "no"?

_____

_____

_____

_____

G. What Is Best for You?

Continue as you are and check the following possibilities:

❏ Leaves his wife and marries you.

❏ Doesn't leave his wife.

❏ Doesn't leave his wife, but you have children together.

    a.   Pays child support and hides the relationship. ___

    b.   Pays child support and tells his wife. ___

    c.   Takes an active part in raising the child. ___

    d.   If the child is born with serious health problems or develops them, he would participate in its care. ___

❏ End the affair if he does not take steps to leave his marriage by an agreed-upon date.

❏ Ask him to take steps immediately toward leaving his marriage.

❏ Start to build your life apart from him and leave at a predetermined time.

❏ End the relationship now.

What conclusions can you come to about your affair?

_____

_____

_____

_____

_____

_____

References

Andersen, Christopher. *Jack and Jackie*. New York: William Morrow and Company, Inc. (1996).

Ansbacher, Heinz, and Rowena Ansbacher, eds. *The Individual Psychology of Alfred Adler*. New York: Basic Books (1956).

Beck, Aaron T. *Love Is Never Enough*. New York: Harper and Row (1988).

Brenner, Marie. *Great Dames*. New York: Three Rivers Press (2000).

Bowen, Murray. *Family Therapy in Clinical Practice*. New York: Jason Aronson (1978).

Brammer, Lawrence, et al. "Intervention Strategies for Coping with Transitions." *The Counseling Psychologist*: 9 (2), 19–36 (1981).

Brown, Emily. *Patterns of Infidelity and Their Treatment*. New York: Brunner/Mazel (1991).

Burns, David. *Feeling Good*. New York: William Morrow and Company (1998).

———. *The Feeling Good Handbook*. New York: William Morrow and Company (1989).

———. *Intimate Connections*. New York: William Morrow and Company (1985).

Burrell, Paul. *A Royal Duty*. New York: Signet Books (2004).

Carnes, Patrick. *Out of the Shadows*. Center City, Minneapolis: Hazelden (1992).

Cato, Leigh. *The Other Woman*. Atlanta, GA: The Longstreet Press (1996).

Clinton, Bill. *My Life*. New York: Alfred A. Knopf (2004).

Cooper, Al, ed. *Cybersex: The Dark Side of the Force*. New York: Brunner-Routledge (2000).

Davis, Martha, Elizabeth R. Eshelman, and Matthew McKay. *Relaxation and Stress Reduction Workbook*. California: New Harbinger Publications (1982).

Elliott, T. "Counseling Adults from Schlossberg's Adaptation Model." *American Mental Health Counselors Association Journal*: 7 (3) (July 1985).

Ellis, Albert. *A New Guide to Rational Living*. North Hollywood, CA: Wilshire Books (1975).

Fogarty, T. F. "The Distancer and the Pursuer," *The Family*. Vol. 7 No 1, 11–16 (1979).

Fonda, Jane. *My Life So Far*. New York: Random House (2005).

Frankl, Viktor E. *Man's Search For Meaning*. New York: Washington Square Press (1963).

Glass, S., and T. Wright. "Restructuring Marriages after the Trauma of Infidelity," in Kim Halford and Howard J. Markham, eds., *Clinical Handbook of Marriage and Couples Intervention*. New York: John Wiley & Sons, 471–507 (1996).

Glass, Shirley. *NOT "Just Friends."* New York: The Free Press (2003).

Gottman, John. *The Seven Principles for Making Marriage Work*. New York: Three Rivers Press (1999).

Gough, Elissa. *The Other Woman's Guide to Infidelity: The Journal for Women in Affairs with Married Men*. Cincinnati: Face Reality, Inc. (1998).

Greenfield, David. *Virtual Addiction*, Oakland, CA: New Harbinger Publications, Inc. (1999).

Grosskopf, Barry. *Forgive Your Parents, Heal Yourself.* New York: Free Press (1999).

Halper, Jan. *Desperate Men: The Truth about Successful Men.* New York: Warner Books, Inc. (1988).

Halpern, Howard M. *How to Break Your Addiction to a Person.* New York: Bantam Books (1982).

Heyman, C. David. *A Woman Named Jackie.* New York: Carol Communications (1989).

Heyn, Dalma. *The Erotic Silence of the American Wife.* New York: Turtle Bay (1992).

Holmes, T. H., and R. Rahe, "The Social Readjustment Rating Scale," *Journal of Psychosomatic Research,* II, 213–218 (1967).

Hopson, B., and, J. Adams, "Toward an Understanding of Transitions: Defining Some Boundaries of Transition." Hopson, B., and J. Adams. (eds.) *Transitions: Understanding and Managing Personal Change.* Montclair, NJ: Allenhald and Osmund (1977).

Hyde, Margaret O., and E. Forsyth. *AIDS: What Does It Mean to You?* New York: Walker and Co. (1987).

Imber-Black, Evan, J. Roberts, and R. Whiting. *Rituals in Families and Family Therapy.* New York: W. W. Norton and Company (1988).

Jacobson, Edmund. *Progressive Relaxation.* Chicago: University of Chicago Press (1959).

Janus, Samuel, and Cynthia Janus. *The Janus Report on Sexual Behavior.* New York: John Wiley & Sons, Inc. (1993).

Kern, Roy M., K. B. Matheny, and D. Patterson. *A Case for Adlerian Counseling.* Chicago: The Alfred Adler Institute of Chicago (1979).

Kubler-Ross, Elisabeth. *On Death and Dying.* New York: Macmillan (1969).

Leaming, Barbara. *Mrs. Kennedy.* New York: The Free Press (2001).

Levine, Deborah. *The Joy of Cybersex.* New York: Ballantine Publishing Group (1998).

Loring, Honey, and J. Birch. *You're On . . . Teaching Assertiveness and Communication Skills.* Putney, VT: Stress Press (1984).

Luskin, Frederic. *Forgive for Good: A Proven Prescription for Health and Happiness.* New York: HarpersCollins (2002).

Maheu, Marlene, and Rona Subotnik. *Infidelity on the Internet: Virtual Relationships and Real Betrayal.* Naperville, IL: Sourcebooks, Inc. (2001).

Maltz, Maxwell. *Psycho-Cybernetics.* New York: Prentice-Hall, Inc. (1960).

McGoldrick, Monica, and R. Gerson. *Genograms in Family Assessment.* New York: W. W. Norton and Company (1985).

Michael, Robert, John H. Gagnon, Edward O. Laumann, and Gina Kolata. *Sex in America.* New York: Warner Books, Inc. (1994).

Miner, Nanette, and Sandi Terri. *This Affair Is Over!!* Bristol, CT: BVC Publishing (1996).

Morton, Andrew. *Monica's Story.* New York: St. Martin's Press (1999).

Neuman, M. Gary. *Emotional Infidelity: How to Affair-Proof Your Marriage and 10 Other Secrets to a Great Relationship.* New York: Three Rivers Press (2001).

Osborn, S. M., and G. G. Harris. *Assertive Training for Women.* Springfield, IL.: Charles C. Thomas (1975).

Parkes, Colin, and Robert Weiss. *Recovery from Bereavement.* New York: Basic Books (1983).

Pittman, Frank. *Man Enough: Fathers, Sons, and the Search for Masculinity.* New York: Berkley Publishing Group (1993).

———. *Private Lies.* New York: W. W. Norton (1989).

Reinisch, June. *The Kinsey Institute New Report On Sex.* New York: St. Martin's Press (1990).

Richardson, Laurel. *The New Other Woman: Contemporary Single Women in Affairs with Married Men.* New York: The Free Press (1985).

Rubenstein, Carin, and Phil Shaver. *In Search of Intimacy.* New York: Delacorte (1974).

Scarf, Maggie. *Intimate Partners.* New York: Random House (1987).

Schlossberg, Nancy. "A Model for Analyzing Human Adaptation to Transitions," *Counseling Psychologist,* 9 (2), 2–18 (1981).

———. *Counseling Adults in Transition.* New York: Springer (1984).

Schneider, Jennifer. *Back from Betrayal.* New York: Ballantine Books (1990).

Schneider, Jennifer, and Robert Weiss. *Cybersex Exposed: Simple Fantasy or Obsession?* Center City, MN: Hazelton (2001).

Shainess, Natalie. *Sweet Suffering: Woman as Victim.* New York: Pocket Books (1984).

Shapiro, Allison. "Fantasy Affairs or Dangerous Liaisons?: Relations in the Cyberworld," *Family Therapy News,* 12–13 (February 1997).

Shulman, Bernard H., *Contributions to Individual Psychology.* Chicago: The Alfred Adler Institute of Chicago (1973).

Smith, Shader, Diane. *Undressing Infidelity.* MA: Adams Media, Inc. (2005).

Starr, Kenneth. *The Starr Report: The Findings of Independent Counsel Kenneth W. Starr on President Clinton and the White House Scandals.* New York: PublicAffairs (1998).

Sternberg, Robert. *The Triangle of Love: Intimacy, Passion, and Commitment.* New York: Basic Books (1988).

Subotnik, Rona. "Using Genograms in Family Therapy." *www.Here2 listen.com* (October 2000).

Subotnik, Rona, and Gloria Harris. *Surviving Infidelity: Making Decisions, Recovering from the Pain,* 3rd ed. Massachusetts: Adams Media, Inc. (2005).

Titelman, Peter, ed. *Clinical Applications of Bowen Family Systems Therapy*. New York: Haworth Press (1998).

———. *Emotional Cutoff: Bowen Family Systems Theory Perspectives*. Binghamton, New York: The Hayworth Clinical Practice Press (2003).

Tobias, Sheila. *Faces of Feminism*. New York: Westview Press (1997).

Trotter, Robert J. "The Three Faces of Love," *Psychology Today*, 47–54 (September 1986).

Tuch, Richard. *The Single Woman–Married Man Syndrome*. Northvale, NJ: Jason Aronson, Inc. (2002).

Tyler, Anne. *The Amateur Marriage*. New York: Random House (2004).

Vanderbilt, Gloria. *It Seemed Important at the Time: A Romance Memoir*. New York: Simon and Schuster (2004).

Vaughan, Peggy. *The Monogamy Myth*. New York: New Market Press (1989).

———. *Dear Peggy: Peggy Vaughan Answers Questions about Extramarital Affairs*. La Jolla, CA: Dialog Press (1999).

Wallerstein, Judith S., and Joan B. Kelly. *Surviving the Breakup: How Children and Parents Cope with Divorce*. New York: Basic Books (1996).

Weil, Bonnie. *Adultery: The Forgivable Sin*. New York: Birch Lane Press (1993).

Weiss, Robert. *Marital Separation*. New York: Basic Books (1975).

———. *Going It Alone*. New York: Basic Books (1979).

Wharfe, Ken. *Diana: Closely Guarded Secret*. New York: Michael O'Mara Books Limited (2002).

Young, K. S. "Internet Addiction: The Emergence of a New Clinical Disorder," *CyberPsychology and Behavior,* 1 (3), 237–244 (1998).

Index

About the Author

RONA B. SUBOTNIK is a licensed marriage and family therapist, and is a clinical member of both the California and American Associations of Marriage and Family Therapists. She received her M.A. in counseling from Trinity College in Washington, D.C.

She is the coauthor of one of the bestselling books on infidelity, *Surviving Infidelity: Making Decisions, Recovering from the Pain*, published in 1994 and updated in its second edition in 1999, and third edition in 2005. She is also the coauthor of *Infidelity on the Internet: Virtual Relationships and Real Betrayal*, published in 2001. She has a work-in-progress chapter for *Family Therapy and Counseling Series* for professionals to be published in 2006. She was a featured monthly columnist for the Internet psychology Web site called *www.Here2Listen.com*. She has appeared on the *Leeza Show* on national television, and on Canadian radio and Radio Free Europe discussing infidelity. She has been interviewed for major newspapers and magazines, such as the *Chicago Tribune*, *San Diego Union Tribune*, and *Newsweek*.

For eight years, Mrs. Subotnik worked at A Woman's Place, an innovative counseling center that is a government program of the Commission for Women of Montgomery County, Maryland. There she conducted individual therapy sessions, and designed and led numerous workshops and counseling groups for women, such as Surviving Infidelity.

Mrs. Subotnik also taught in the graduate studies department at Trinity College, and the Women's Studies Extension Program at Mt. Vernon College in Washington, D.C.

She has served as a member of the Commission on the Status of Women on San Diego's Committee on Sexual Harassment for three years, and its Committee on Domestic Violence for one year.

Mrs. Subotnik has been in private practice for fourteen years in California. She is married and has three adult children. Currently, she lives in Palm Desert, where she is in private practice.

Visit her Web site at *www.survivinginfidelity.com*.